D1076506

is for **Sheep**

– getting ready for phonics

Ros Bayley, Helen Bilton, Lynn Broadbent,
Marion Dowling, Margaret Edgington,
Janet Evans, Judith Harries, Jennie Lindon,
Janet Moyles, Linda Pound, Kym Scott,
Judith Stevens, Penny Tassoni

Edited by Sally Featherstone

Preface

L is for Sheep was Ros Bayley's idea. She began to share it with others in 2005, just as the latest debate about phonics was gaining momentum. Word of a proposed work which would draw together the views of a group of influential early years writers and thinkers quickly spread, until there were fourteen of us involved in the project, each willing to contribute their expertise to a book about what should come before systematic programmes in early reading development.

We all had stories about young children's responses to formal phonic work which might serve for a title, but in the end L is for Sheep won! We are sure many readers will have anecdotes like the following one, illustrated on the book cover.

When I was head of a nursery/infant school, five year old Shane came to show me his work. It was a phonic worksheet of words that start with the 'L' sound. I complimented him on the accurate colouring and the careful way he had copied the words next to the pictures on the sheet. I then made the mistake of asking him to read the words next to the pictures!

I said, "L is for...?"

Shane said, "Lemon."

"Good," I said. "Now, the next one. L is for...?"

"Lolly," said Shane, looking pleased with himself.

"Good boy!" I said. "And now the last one. L is for...?"

Shane thought for a moment before, his face lighting up, he bellowed, "L is for sheep!"

Shane was not really learning. He was jumping through hoops, trying to come up with responses that would please his teacher based on an imperfect understanding of the relationship between words and their initial sounds. The worksheet was making no contribution to his learning. It was simply exposing what he didn't know. How much better it would have been for him to work with real objects and to sort them according to what he knew, understood and thought, making a judgement and saying the name of each object aloud as he collected all the ones starting with 'l' in his basket. In Shane's case, the lamb would have stayed on the carpet – a focus for adult praise in thinking and listening and a starting point for the next stage in his learning.

Historically for many children phonic work has been as relevant to real experiences as it was for Shane, focusing on worksheets and other empty activities rather than employing a multi-sensory approach coherent with what we now know makes sense for young learners. The fourteen contributors to this book, all of them

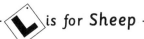

experienced early years practitioners and many involved in higher education and the provision of training, consultancy and guidance, have written this book as a shared statement of their beliefs.

L is for Sheep is about language development in the early years and how practitioners can best prepare children for the structured teaching of reading, and particularly for the approach called Synthetic Phonics. We have each written from the standpoint of what we know to be true, based on our reading, research, discussions with practitioners and teachers, and above all on our personal interactions with children. Our beliefs affect what we advise practitioners to do. Some of us have written short essays on relevant topics where we have a specialism, some of us have written about good practice in the teaching of reading and writing, and others have added ideas for activities to help you to provide that 'rich diet of language development' (*The Rose Report*, 2006). These are all intended for individuals and small groups of children, and we hope readers will select those which best meet the needs of the children they know. The activities are suitable for children in the Foundation Stage and for those in Key Stage 1 who you feel need more practice in listening and interpreting sounds. There is also guidance on how you might adapt the indoor and outdoor environments to support the development of phonological awareness in your own setting or school.

Sally Featherstone

Editor's Note

We have used 'practitioner' throughout this book as an inclusive term to indicate any adult who cares for a child other than their own – nursery nurse or assistant, teacher, classroom assistant, childminder, day carer and so on.

Pronouns are a problem – and so is gender! Rather than tediously repeat 'or him' whenever we mention 'her' and 'or her' every time we mention 'him' we have referred to the child as masculine throughout, unless the sense of the text requires a precise assignation of gender. So when applied to children please take 'him' and 'his' to include 'her' and 'hers'. Similarly, despite having had the privilege of meeting a number of excellent male nursery workers, we have referred to practitioners throughout as 'her'.

These arbitrary decisions have been taken in the interests of readability and clarity; if they offend anyone we apologise.

L is for **Sheep**

Contents

Introduction: Sally Featherstone   1

Part 1

First things first: Marion Dowling   11

A sofa full of talkers: Jennie Lindon   21

Tuning in: Penny Tassoni   37

Part 2

Introduction to part 2: Sally Featherstone   47

Sounds good to me! Linda Pound   51

Why the fuss about phonics? Margaret Edgington   61

Is everybody ready? Janet Moyles   69

Reading for writing: Janet Evans   83

Part 3

Introduction to part 3: Sally Featherstone   97

Miss, I want that bike: Helen Bilton   107

Writing and mark making: Penny Tassoni   115

Tune into sound as you move around: Ros Bayley & Lynn Broadbent   125

Stages, not ages: Kym Scott & Judith Stevens   135

Learning to listen with puppets: Ros Bayley & Lynn Broadbent   155

Sound it out: Judith Harries   165

Tailpiece: Sally Featherstone   177

Glossary   180

L is for **Sheep**

Introduction

This introduction, and the book itself, are written for practitioners and teachers in the Foundation Stage and early Key Stage One who are attempting to make sense of phonics teaching in the Early Years. As is clear from the current discussion in the profession, in politics, in the media and with parents, opinions vary widely on the best time, the best method and the best context for introducing structured programmes of phonics teaching.

The writers of *L is For Sheep* are united in supporting the following statement from *The Independent Review of the Teaching of Early Reading* (The Rose Report, DfES. March 2006):

... the new Early Years Foundation Stage and the renewed framework should make sure that best practice for beginner readers provides them with a rich curriculum that fosters all four interdependent strands of language: speaking, listening, reading and writing. The indications are that far more attention needs to be given, right from the start, to promoting speaking and listening skills to make sure that children build a good stock of words, learn to listen attentively and speak clearly and confidently. Speaking and listening, together with reading and writing, are prime communication skills that are central to children's intellectual, social and emotional development. All these skills are drawn upon and promoted by high quality, systematic phonic work.

And:

... the introduction of phonic work should always be a matter for principled, professional judgement based on structured observations and assessments of children's capabilities.

We are however more concerned that a definition of what 'high quality, systematic phonic work' looks like is less clear. We are also committed to ensuring that the 'principled professional judgement' of practitioners and teachers in defining such a programme remains enshrined in the amended legislation which results from the Report and in future practice in the Early Years Foundation Stage and Key Stage 1.

Learning to read English is a complex, sometimes daunting challenge for children and their teachers. The sensitive process of attuning voices, ears, eyes and minds takes time and practice. A single method may not suit every child, and the 'hands-on' sensory approach of the curriculum for under fives is an essential element in any successful reading experience. The guiding principles of the

National Curriculum apply just as strongly to any planned programme of reading activity as they do to other curriculum subjects and aspects.

Practitioners will welcome The Rose Report for its emphasis on 'a broad, rich language experience'; they will be less confident that the large group teaching sessions will be effective, particularly for four and young five year olds. Of course a large group session can be made 'multisensory and active' but engagement and learning is likely to be superficial for many members of the group, particularly the youngest and many boys. Of course the large group sessions will be well managed and orderly and many children will appear to be engaged, but the engagement will be adult directed rather than child initiated and will often have been arranged at a time when the children have to be removed from child initiated learning at just the stage when deep involvement has begun. Children take time to get really involved in their own self-chosen activities, and curtailing this play just as it has begun to enter a deeply involved stage will be frustrating at best and infuriating at worst!

As writers and early years specialists, we accept that there have been some surprising results from programmes where large group, adult led and formally arranged sessions appear to have resulted in gains in word recognition, sound to symbol match and phonic awareness. However, we would wish to ask, 'What is the cost to child initiated learning of adopting this method? How many children have been frustrated in their chosen play by the imposition of structured sessions, and how much damage have we done to the fragile confidence of many boys and some girls by presenting them with an activity which they CAN do but would probably not choose to do?'

We have addressed these and many more interlinked factors affecting the development of phonological awareness in the three parts of *L is For Sheep*.

Part 1: The earliest learning

Children in their earliest years are making learning links in their brains at a faster rate than they will ever do again. The learning of babies and young children is the foundation for everything they later become, and it is well known that learning is most effective in a stimulating environment, full of adults who are interested in them as individuals. Such learning cannot be 'programmed'. It is an organic process, where playful and positive exchanges of song, sound, facial expression and touch between adults and children, and between children themselves, form a basis for skilful communication.

Unfortunately, some children do not have the rich communication environment essential for developing these key skills; and there is a view among professionals that children as a whole are entering settings and schools with less developed communication skills than in previous generations. Early years

practitioners working with under fives are very conscious of the need to observe each child closely and provide additional support for those who have not had stimulating and language rich experiences. The guidance for Birth to Three Matters states:

... all children have from birth a need to develop, learning through interaction with people and exploration of the world around them. For some children, this development may be at risk because of difficulties with communication and interaction, cognition and learning, behavioural, emotional and social development or sensory and physical development. (Birth to Three Matters, DfES SureStart: 2004)

Good practitioners take time and trouble to compensate for early deficits and emerging needs.

Those who work in the early years (and most would accept that the period from birth to seven is a crucial stage) must understand both the needs of young learners and the power of adults in ensuring that needs are met. The framework and guidance for birth to three and the Foundation Stage has taken almost a decade to research, construct, and establish. It enshrines a commitment to a developmentally appropriate environment within which children can play and learn at a pace and through activities which are truly relevant to them as individuals.

Children deepen their understanding by playing, talking, observing, planning, questioning, experimenting, testing, repeating, reflecting and responding to adults and to each other...Practitioners must be able to observe and respond appropriately to children, informed by a knowledge of how children develop and learn and a clear understanding of the next steps in their development in learning. (Curriculum Guidance for the Foundation Stage, DfES: 2000)

Guidance and training have resulted in enormous improvements in practice among professionals and done much to assure appropriate experiences for children. We have no reason to believe that the guidance for the Early Years Foundation Stage (EYFS) will change the emphasis on high quality professional practice, knowledge of child development and the ability to plan on the basis of observing individual children. However, there is a risk that the ever increasing pressure for results and the desire to 'close the gap' between children who succeed and those who are less successful will affect the balance of activities in early years settings and classes, moving away from the highly effective practice identified in research and supported in DfES guidance to Local Authorities. Many of the practitioners who work with this guidance put much time and effort into securing appropriate resources, equipment and space, where children can learn through play, supported by adults who are 'partners in their sustained shared thinking' (The Effective Provision of Pre-School Education [EPPE], University of London. 2005).

EPPE and REPEY (Research into Effective Pedagogy in the Early Years) have explored the characteristics of different kinds of provision and examined children's development in early years settings from age three, and their progress in school to the end of Key Stage 1. The study has recently been extended to the end of Key Stage 2. REPEY/EPPE have been able to identify the aspects of early years provision which have a positive impact on children's attainment, progress and development and so provide guidance on good practice. Significant points to consider from this research are the importance of the practitioner's role in balancing adult-led and child-initiated activities, the need to engage in 'sustained shared thinking' and the kinds of interactions that will guide but not dominate children's thinking. (*KEEP: Key Elements of Effective Practice, DfES. 2005*)

In Part 1, the early stages of the development of language and listening are explored in contributions by Marion Dowling, Jennie Lindon and Penny Tassoni, who give their experienced insight into the lives and learning of very young children. This section will give practitioners working with under fives, and their colleagues in Key Stage 1, information about the environment and exchanges babies and young children need in order to become skilful speakers and listeners. This section also underlines the vital importance of involving parents in the language development of their children – not through commercial programmes or heavily marketed video and electronic toys, but by spending time with their children in the small conversations, songs, rhymes and stories that enrich their children's lives and learning.

Part 2: The current debate and learning to read

The teaching of reading, and the place of phonics within reading is a contentious topic with strongly held views on all sides. Not only is there a 'phonics v. no phonics' debate, but there are also contrasting views on 'phonics early v. phonics later', and 'analytical' v. 'synthetic' phonics. There is also disagreement about the optimum time for children to be involved in a structured programme of phonic teaching and the most suitable size of groups for effective early learning.

Learning to read is a complex process, and the education profession has been engaged in unravelling its intricacies since schools began. Research, theory, opinion, belief, prejudice, practice, personal experience and commerce have all played a part in their approaches. There has been a regular revisiting of the benefits of 'whole word', 'phonic', 'look and say', 'apprenticeship', and many other methodologies which have been adopted, sometimes adapted and then abandoned. People have tried to teach babies to read, the Initial Teaching Alphabet promised to simplify decoding and bring the rapid acquisition of reading skills to every child, reading schemes and programmes with widely differing approaches have been

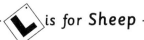

launched, usually with associated promises to accelerate, improve, remediate or deepen the experience of learning to read. Methods have been described as 'fun', 'motivating', 'systematic', 'proven', 'researched', and many have had some success, particularly when combined with the enthusiasm of dedicated teachers, prepared to put their time, energy and expertise into searching for the Holy Grail of the perfect method of making one of the most complex and confusing languages in the world comprehensible to beginning readers.

Over time, a majority of teachers arrived at the conclusion that because children are different, a single system was unlikely to work for everyone. A range of approaches was needed, from which individuals could select. This view was confirmed by their observation and experience of the many ways children use to help them make sense of print. In this mixed economy of reading, the development of phonological awareness was usually a key constituent, and was often imaginatively and comprehensively offered to children as part of a rich range of language experiences. At its best it offered enough of everything to provide a menu from which children could take the ingredients they needed to make their own recipe for reading. However, in some cases the phonological and word recognition elements were not in the right proportions or not presented consistently or appropriately enough to motivate individuals or groups. The result was that some children became disengaged from the process, and rather than becoming self sufficient and autonomous readers they needed more support as they grew older. These children – the majority, but not all, seem to be boys – were cut adrift and some failed to learn to read altogether.

The National Literacy Strategy was intended to achieve an appropriate balance between the key elements of reading. After an over-prescriptive initial phase the strategy settled down to a more flexible model, where individual teachers and schools were able to look closely at the children in their care and tailor their approach to fit their circumstances. At its best this has worked very well by allowing teachers and schools considerable flexibility. However it has not been without its dangers. Some schools and teachers confuse freedom to use their judgement with a random 'pick and mix' approach, which at best hits the target only sometimes and at worst misses the needs of most children altogether. The result is reflected in the Rose Report, where a perceived need to return to 'fidelity to the programme' is in danger of destroying the best work of the Literacy Strategy and its associated support materials by abandoning a multi-faceted approach in favour of 'one size fits all'.

In Part 2, Linda Pound, Margaret Edgington, Janet Moyles and Janet Evans give their personal and professional views of the place of phonics in the early years curriculum and in the teaching of reading.

Part 3: What does 'a rich curriculum that fosters all four interdependent strands of language: speaking, listening, reading and writing' (Rose, 2006) look like?

Whatever method is used in the early stages of teaching children to read, we are convinced that inspiring an enduring enjoyment of reading should be a key objective. This can be endangered both by an overly formal approach in the early years and by a failure to teach decoding. (House of Commons Education and Skills Committee, Teaching Children to Read; Eighth Report of Session 2004-05)

Perhaps phonics has not been well taught in the past. Perhaps it is indeed true that teaching phonics has been 'a neglected or weak feature of teaching' (Rose: 2006), but if the recommendations of the Rose Report are interpreted too rigidly by civil servants, members of national and local government and some managers of settings, and taken as encouragement to impose an over-formal structure for teaching on young children and their teachers, there could be a disastrous regression in educational thinking and practice, which could affect a whole generation of children. It would be sensible to take note of the reservations expressed in the Report:

...findings from different research programmes are sometimes contradictory or inconclusive, and often call for further studies to test tentative findings. (Rose: 2006)

A common feature of many new projects is that it is easy to identify and celebrate success in the short term, particularly when these projects have been implemented by charismatic and enthusiastic individuals. It is more difficult to measure the long term effects, how – or even whether – changes in attitude have any far reaching impact on children's learning, and the extent to which short term gains are carried forward to affect interest and motivation over a long period. In a worrying echo of some of the 'cure all' recipes we all know from the past, we are in danger of falling into the trap of being bedazzled into implementing across the country an approach that may have been tested in only a small group of highly supported, highly motivated schools.

Many practitioners may not read The Rose Report in its entirety, getting their information from the media, or from commercial sources eager to promote programmes and materials promising a 'quick fix'. Others may read into the more extreme media coverage a condemnation of everything they have done before – including much good practice. As a result they may fail to take full note of some of the detail buried in the Report, particularly the encouragement to professionals to use their judgement. For example:

is for Sheep

For most children, high quality, systematic phonic work should start by the age of five, taking full account of professional judgments of children's developing abilities and the need to embed this work within a broad and rich curriculum. This should be preceded by pre-reading activities that pave the way for such work to start. (Rose: 2006)

Educators are used to being bombarded by government initiatives. They have survived the implementation of an ever evolving National Curriculum and its associated assessment, league tables, inspection and self evaluation, new professional standards and expectations and a raft of sometimes conflicting guidance on the processes of learning and teaching. The early years sector, and particularly the Foundation Stage, has been particularly affected by national initiatives. In 1999 there was no Foundation Stage: Reception classes were deemed 'quasi Key Stage 1' with corresponding expectations; Nursery classes were in a sort of limbo, and the vast range of providers outside the maintained sector were hardly considered part of education at all, being deemed the 'care sector'. By 2002 practitioners had a statutory Foundation Stage with its own guidance and assessment arrangements, implemented and inspected against national standards in all types of settings including day nurseries, pre-schools and child minding networks. By 2008 there will be a statutory birth to five framework (the Early Years Foundation Stage) with a set of national standards and guidance which should allow all practitioners to provide a personalised education for children from very soon after birth.

One of the most significant factors in this huge investment in early learning has been to include a wide range of practitioners (including trained teachers) in shared discussion, professional development and visits across all sectors of this newly amalgamated Key Stage. In these settings, hardly mentioned in the Rose Report, huge efforts have been made to support a vast number of practitioners from all sorts of backgrounds and in all sorts of environments to raise their expectations of themselves as professionals in improving both their knowledge of learning and their interactions with children. An insensitive and over-prescriptive interpretation of The Rose Report could do immeasurable damage to this emerging host of practitioners. They are working in a profession where the annual turnover of staff is sometimes as high as 50%, where pressure from parents can divert the best professional practice, and where training of the huge workforce is a never ending task. The managers of settings in the private, voluntary and independent sectors, many now accommodating four and five year olds in their groups, may see the recommendations of the report as an indication that 'younger is better' in the race to learn words. In their natural desire to give their children a flying start, and following the likely pressure from some parents, they may be tempted to adopt inappropriate methods in settings that have only recently been weaned away from worksheets and unsuitable commercial programmes.

Children in their early years need activities which are meaningful to them, so any programme must be personal to the children in the group. It is well known that young children learn better in pairs and small groups, and that large group sessions offer them a much less effective context for learning. They also benefit from a multi-sensory approach. Some commercial programmes do include movement, music and rhyme, appealing to all senses and learning styles, but a programme always has a 'direction' a 'next level', a 'Book 2', implying that moving on is important, when research tells us that children need repetition, familiarity and sensitive challenge based on real knowledge of their needs. Over emphasis by the government on a formal, tightly structured, inflexible approach would fail to recognise the key characteristics of early learning and risk excluding just the group who would most benefit from relevant materials and high quality training packages. In their absence, practitioners working outside the maintained sector may well be tempted by untested commercial packages, including table based or pencil and paper activities.

In Part 3 another group of well known and recognised early years trainers, writers and advisers offer practitioners a wealth of simple ideas for putting theory into practice in settings and schools. The aim is to provide a range of ways to increase the impact of familiar activities and resources, focusing them clearly on helping children to develop phonological awareness and the skills of listening and speaking. The intention is to reinforce and expand the good practice which can be seen in many early years settings, where active, multi-sensory programmes are already in place and where children learn with enthusiasm. The activities presented here are rooted in the writers' experience of high quality early years practice; some are based on Playing with Sounds, a valuable recent addition to the resources for the Foundation Stage, which has been the focus for training across the whole range of practitioners and settings. They have the advantage of engaging children in the literacy process though action, song, rhythm and sound. They also take account of significant research in the USA, which has found that systematic phonic teaching does indeed have a significant effect on learning to read, but is most effective when used together with two other elements:

> *Systematic phonics instruction, when combined with language activities and individual tutoring, may triple the effect of phonics alone. (Teaching Children to Read: The Fragile Link Between Science and Federal Education Policy, National Institute for Early Education Research and Rutgers University. 2003)*

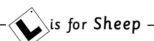

In order of their appearance, Helen Bilton, Penny Tassoni, Ros Bayley, Lynn Broadbent, Kym Scott, Judith Stevens and Judith Harries have put together collections of ideas for practice in developing phonological awareness in young children. We hope you will enjoy them – we know the children will! In making use of them and in all your work we ask you to keep in mind that it is you, the professional who makes the decision on when a child is ready for the next step, a variation on a game, a new challenge or a structured programme. You and your colleagues are the ones who know the children best and can decide on what to plan. You are the people who know the child's parents, their family situation, their community and their background. Match this intimate knowledge by learning all you can about how children develop, how reading happens, the skills the children need and the activities that are meaningful to them. Use both to argue the case for an appropriate early years curriculum where children are engaged, excited and motivated to continue their learning journey.

Sally Featherstone

L is for Sheep

Marion Dowling
First things first

Marion Dowling has spent all of her varied career working in Early Years. She was in turn headteacher of a maintained nursery school, an adviser in two large shire authorities and a member of Her Majesty's Inspectorate. Since 1994 she has worked independently as a consultant on local and national initiatives. She contributed evidence to the Audit Commission study on pre-school provision 'Counting to Five', was involved in initial training for the Foundation Stage and a local evaluator for Early Excellence Centres.

Marion publishes regularly in early years journals and is the author of several books, including 'Young Children's Personal, Social and Emotional Development'. She is currently consultant to the journal '3-13' and President of Early Education, a national charity which supports practitioners and parents in providing high quality care and education for young children. Marion has recently acted as project manager for the Early Education Project 'Supporting Young Children's Sustained Shared Thinking'.

In *First things first*, Marion explores characteristics in the personal growth of babies and young children that influence effective language learning, and examines how these characteristics are best supported. She argues that communication with and the affirmation of close adults in a relationship of support and trust is essential to emotional and mental wellbeing. Children who enjoy such an environment are well placed to learn effectively, including mastering reading. Those who are unfortunate enough to lack it might well never catch up.

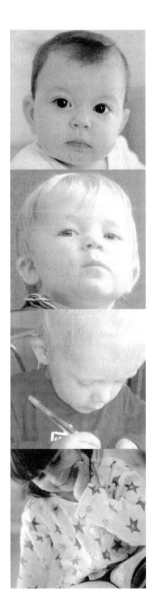

Parents and early years practitioners have a huge privilege; they help to shape the lives of babies and young children. We are now only too aware of how experiences in early years can influence lives later on for good or ill, and so with the privilege comes a great responsibility to 'get it right' for children. Naturally, responsible adults want young children to learn well and make progress. Moreover, we recognise that access to the world of words, both spoken and written, is every child's entitlement.

But first things first; our priority must be to tune into the child. We need to recognise all that makes each child a unique person and use that to nurture the positive aspects of their personal development. We know now that babies are equipped for language at birth, but there are conditions to be met in order for this potential to be realised. Studies show strongly that that feelings really matter in developing our young children's learning capacities. This is hardly surprising, because the type of person we become colours all else we do in life. It is no accident that focusing on and improving young children's emotional and communication skills has been set as one of the two main current targets for SureStart units.

> *All areas of learning and development are intricately intertwined. Young children develop and learn holistically and their emotional and social development seems to form the bedrock of other areas. (Birth to Three Matters: a review of the literature, DfES. 2003. p69)*

This first chapter explores characteristics in the personal growth of babies and young children that influence effective language learning, and examines how these characteristics are best supported.

Becoming confident and pro-active: 'I can learn'

In a world that expects so much of them, children need to become confident and self-assured from an early age. Although they may be born with different personality traits, children's levels of confidence are highly influenced by early experiences, successes and failures, the thoughts that children have about themselves and other people's reactions to them.

> *At the core of 'A Strong Child' lies development of the baby's and young child's sense of personal and group identity and the ways this can be acknowledged and affirmed by those around him/her. (Birth to Three Matters: a Strong Child, DfES/SureStart. 2002)*

Children begin to recognise themselves from an early age. Babies start to build this picture from the way in which they are regarded and treated by the people closest to them. When babies start their lives having at least one parent or carer with whom they have a close link or attachment this is a vital ingredient in

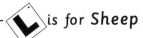

helping them to recognise that they matter. Every day that this important person can be with the baby, to discover him, meet his needs, give him pleasure and show pleasure in him, help him to know her, will contribute to an investment of confidence and inner calm. If babies receive this nurture during the first few months of life they become able to understand, think, communicate and learn.

All change can be stressful and the move from home to a group setting for a child under three is potentially traumatic. When babies and small children come to separate from their parents, the essential need is to appoint a key person with whom the child can make a similar attachment. The transition from home to an early years setting needs to be entirely geared to the individual to ensure continuity of approach and experience. The success of the transition is dependent on the key person, who becomes the child's point of reference in the setting. Not only does this person establish a close relationship with the child but also she gets to know him intimately, his worries, his fears and his all-abiding interests. When this happens the key person is able to read the child's behaviour and provide a tailor made response. The child comes to regard her as another significant person in his life, feels relaxed and secure and is open to new experiences. For children under two years this is particularly critical. A recent major study highlights the possible dangers of group care for babies and toddlers, indicating that a lack of individualised attention can jeopardise early social and emotional development (Leach: 2005). Children experience many transitions during their early years of life, and each time they face the prospect of becoming a novice and not knowing what faces them. The same principles of attachment apply even to three and four year olds. A child who feels unknown, unappreciated and useless becomes less, rather than more competent. Until the practitioner enables a sound transition, learning is arrested or takes a backward step.

As toddlers develop they become aware of the way in which other people view them and start to behave accordingly. The loving family and key practitioners have a powerful influence on the child's sense of self. Through their different behaviours these people help the child to know who he is. As the young child goes through the process of establishing his identity he starts to recognise how others see him. The development of self-esteem means placing a value on that identity. Although children don't reach a clear view of their self-worth until they are around six years of age, their earlier experiences provide the basis for them to make a judgement about themselves. Three year old Dean's dad brings over a book to the sofa, hugs his son and asks him to 'show me all the animals because you know this story really well'. Dean grins; he feels affirmed and is keen to share the book with his dad in a warm and loving relationship.

One of the most important gifts we can offer young children is a positive view of themselves. Without this gift they will flounder throughout life and be constantly seeking from others the reassurance they cannot find within. Studies show that young children who have benefited from early strong attachments and affirmation are likely to feel more self-assured in learning.

> *A positive self image and high self esteem gives children the confidence and security to make the most of opportunities, to communicate effectively and to explore the world around them. (Curriculum Guidance for the Foundation Stage, DfES. 2000. p29)*

The way in which young children feel about themselves is reflected in their approach to learning (Dweck and Leggett: 1998; Gerhardt: 2004). In order to learn, children must believe that they are able to do so. Self assured children show a mastery approach – they seek new challenges and are confident that they will succeed even when faced with problems. If this belief is not secured during the early years of life it is unlikely to blossom later. Master learners see themselves as readers and demonstrate reading behaviour early in the nursery. They pick up books and 'read' them to their teddy or to other children. They are keen to share their prowess and point to letters that they recognise from their own name. Other children who have had unhappy early relationships may be less sure of themselves. They are demonised by self- doubt, 'give up' easily and constantly look to others for support. These helpless young learners are the ones who, when struggling to read later on, gaze at the adult, depending on her to supply the words rather than actively engaging with the text for themselves. The great challenge for practitioners is how to support all children to become master learners who adopt an 'I can' approach. This involves looking very closely at each individual, capturing their capabilities and breaking new learning into very small steps to ensure experience of success. This personalised scaffolding is essential. However, progress will only occur if the child feels empowered by the practitioner's open conviction in his capacity to succeed.

Becoming social: I like being and learning with others

We live in a social world, and in the process of growing up children have to learn to be one of a group and to 'rub along' with others. Moreover, the whole basis for young children and adults living and learning together is founded on relationships. Children learn so much by themselves; when they are together with others their learning expands.

Oral Communication underpins all aspects of language and literacy, and Birth to Three Matters reminds us that babies are primed to be social and communicative. A successful early attachment is hugely important for the child's later social

development. If a baby is physically and emotionally close to one person initially (most usually his birth mother) this makes later separation from her more tolerable rather than less. The key person and later other practitioners then pave the way for the child to reach out and communicate with a widening circle.

> When we are babies our brains are socially programmed by the older members of our communities so that we adapt to the particular family and social group we must live among ... rather than holding up flashcards to a baby it would be more appropriate to a baby's stage of development to simply hold him and enjoy him. (Gerhardt. p38)

A child's ability to form good relationships not only enhances his personal development but helps him to make progress intellectually. Social contacts help very young children search out patterns and make sense of their lives. They look to their carer for affirmation and information, and try to imitate the behaviour of older children. They learn a huge range of social skills when they observe members of their family listening, questioning, arguing, manipulating and agreeing. In the Foundation Stage friendships become very important; children develop their group social play, learn to negotiate, compromise and solve altercations among themselves rather than turning to an adult (Broadhead: p49).

Interactions are also very influential during the earliest stages of learning to read. We now recognise that there is a close link between an ability to recognise and match sounds and early success in reading. This includes an early knowledge of nursery rhymes and ability to recognise and produce rhyming words and words beginning with the same letter (Bryant and Bradley: 1985). When parents and practitioners introduce young children to a regular diet of rhymes and songs they will naturally build up these skills. Importantly these experiences should be informal, intimate and fun. Babies and toddlers will enjoy handling books for themselves; they also need familiar adults to mediate for them to help them to explore images and make connections in the context of a loving relationship. When these pleasurable social experiences are repeated regularly, young children come to anticipate that books and stories are something to be enjoyed. There are also many successful examples in schools when older children provide a positive model, forging friendly relationships with younger ones, reading to them and browsing through books together.

Zest - wanting to learn

Babies have a passion to find out. This zest is harnessed by curiosity and powered by the energy to investigate. Contrast this with the sad picture of a two year old who lacks curiosity, or a six year old who appears to have no interest in school and is beginning to show worrying signs of disaffection with learning.

Whatever the causes of this decline we must recognise that although we can make every provision for young children's language development, no-one can make them learn. Moreover, whereas early reading and writing skills may be taught successfully in later life, it is more difficult to bring back to life positive attitudes towards language and literacy. This makes it vital for parents and practitioners to nurture the dispositions that make up a desire to learn.

Very young babies first respond to touch, smell and sound. In the loving arms of a parent a baby relaxes and is responsive to new experiences. The baby quickly starts to recognise familiar faces and makes huge efforts to communicate through eye contact and body gestures. It is behaviour which not only invites response but actually requires it. Babies and toddlers need to experience the reward and stimulus they get from warm and reactive adults. They need to receive that positive feedback and attention when they first reach out to communicate through their actions and then start to experiment with sounds and words: recognition and encouragement gives them a buzz and an incentive to try for more of it! When they start to use spoken language, toddlers, like adults, need a listening ear. More than that, they need adults who give them full and undivided attention and who show that they are genuinely interested in what is being said.

Mastering the early skills of reading and writing is gruelling work for young children and they have to be powerfully inclined to do so. The task for practitioners is to provide the climate, challenge and support which motivates children to invest their energies in this work.

We can become motivated when we feel that we are doing something interesting and succeeding in it, and so it is with children. The younger the child the more important it is to allow them to practice and apply what they know already. Doing more of the same is particularly pleasurable and affirmative for toddlers, but there comes a time to introduce new experiences. By contrast, where adults are over anxious to move on, perhaps to 'instruct' in letter and word recognition, too often they go beyond children's understandings and leave them feeling inept. The precious inclination to learn dissipates quickly when a child is bored or befuddled. Adults need to develop a 'red alert' to the signs of either.

Early reading and writing competencies are bound up with feelings and in sharing these feelings with others. Positive feelings, enjoyment, excitement strongly support learning. As a consequence of enjoying and sharing books individually or in very small groups with an adult, young children become receptive to learning more. In this relaxed context they will look at detail in pictures, ask questions about characters in the text and start to recognise letters in their own name (usually the most significant word for them at this early stage). Children quickly

develop a sense of humour when looking at illustrations and playing with sounds; they relish and remember stories and rhymes that make them laugh.

Feelings can also be detrimental to learning. Young children's emotions are strong and raw. They do not have the benefits of life experience and they face frightening feelings of anger and distress for the first time; some exist on an emotional roller coaster. In these circumstances children can be ruled by their feelings. Negative feelings can affect a child's well being; they can also affect working memory - a measure of the number of things that one can cope with at one time (Rees and Jones, 1996). Although we like to think of young children as carefree, sadly some children, like some adults, are troubled for all sorts of reasons.

Aziz at 4 years and 2 months, already has many worries. He recently arrived as a refugee in this country with his mother and he has found life in this new country very strange. He doesn't know where his father is, and his mother tearfully tells him that they may never see his daddy again. Karen, a little younger, is afraid of going to bed because her brother teases her that a bad man may come at night and take her away.

The scale of concerns for these two children is very different, but in each case the outcomes are similar – agitated and fretful behaviour and an inability to concentrate.

Most adults are able to keep a number of ideas and skills in their minds at one time – many of the things that we once learned laboriously, such as dressing ourselves and making a cup of tea, become automatic. Young children who are new to learning initially find everything a challenge and need all their energies to remember newly acquired skills and understandings. Emotions which are associated with stress, such as anxiety and feelings of insecurity, take up a lot of mental space in the brain; these feelings can 'block' a working memory. As a result a child experiencing these and similarly stressful emotions can become unsure, confused and forgetful, often about things in which he was previously competent.

The move from Reception to Year 1 can prove extremely stressful for some children, particularly if the new regime is unfamiliar. In these circumstances a child becomes a novice once more. Fears of not knowing what to do and of 'getting things wrong' lead to a lack of confidence and subsequent regression in learning. Schools now recognise the need to plan carefully for transition, giving time to exploring and allaying individual fears, providing familiar routines and continuing the play-based learning familiar from the previous setting, while at the same time helping children to savour the excitement of a new experience.

Sometimes children openly express their concerns, but too often their worries fester within and impact on their well-being and learning. Increasingly, early years practitioners find that they have to deal with the distress of children as part of their work. While they cannot (and should not) pry into the child's feelings it is important for children to understand both that an adult recognises when something is wrong for them, and that the adult can be trusted to listen and understand.

Children who are zestful learners are healthy and active. Their young brains thrive with plenty of fresh air, good food, water and rest. But we know that not all young children enjoy these advantages. Many do not start the day with breakfast at home and have limited access to exercise outside. Sleep deprivation is a common problem. Studies from America and the United Kingdom suggest that a large number of children have insufficient rest from babyhood, and this worsens as they get older, Typically children miss the equivalent of one month's sleep a year. This can have a dire affect on the child's physical and mental health; their immune system is likely to become less effective and their behaviour and learning suffers. Some children who show attention deficit behaviours may simply be over-tired (The Times 2 (2.4): 2004. p.9)

Breakfast clubs and the increased use of improved outdoor facilities in early years settings have made a real difference to some children's lives. Parents need to be made aware of the importance a good night's sleep can make to their child's well-being and learning. Moreover, the development of children's centres and the extended day means that provision must be made for children to rest and recharge their batteries.

Sir Christopher Ball stressed in the influential Start Right report that the art of learning is concerned with the 'super skills and attitudes' of which confidence, motivation, and socialisation are the most important. (Ball: para 2.17, 1994) Christopher Ball describes these as the fruits of successful early learning. However they should also be regarded as the seeds that need to take root if we are to grow eager learners who learn from each other and, with zest, have the energy to do so.

References

Ball, C. (1994) Start Right: the Importance of Early Learning. London, RSE.

Bee, P. (2004) Up Until All Hours in *The Times 2, 2.4 p.9*

Broadhead, P. (2004) Early Years Play and Learning. Routledge-Falmer.

Bryant, P.E and Bradley, L. (1985) Children's Reading Problems. Oxford, Blackwell.

David, T., et al (2003) Birth to Three Matters: a Review of the Literature. London, DfES.

Gerhardt, S (2004) Why Love Matters. Bruner-Routledge.

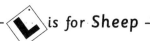
is for **Sheep**

Leach, P., Stein, A. and Sylva, K. (2005) <u>Families, Children and Child Care Study</u>. *Institute for the Study of Children, Families and Social Issues*, London, Birkbeck, University of London.

Rees, D and Shortland-Jones, B (1996) <u>Reading Developmental Continuum, First Steps Project</u>. Government of Western Australia, Rigby Heimemann.

QCA (2000) <u>Curriculum Guidance for the Foundation Stage</u>. London, QCA/DfEE.

Sure Start (2003) <u>Birth to three Matters: A Framework to Support Children in their Earliest Years</u>. London, DfES.

Jennie Lindon
A sofa full of talkers

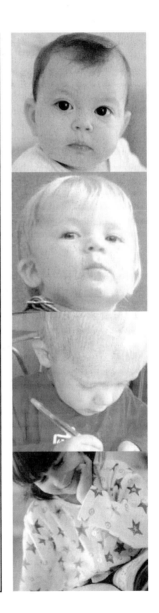

Jennie Lindon is an early childhood specialist, whose background is in child psychology. Jennie has thirty years of experience of working with early years and play services for children and their families. Based in South London, she runs her own business as an independent trainer, consultant and author. Jennie has become increasingly concerned about the pressures on early years practitioners in all types of provision.

An established author, Jennie has had more than twenty books published. Recent titles include *Understanding Children's Play* (Nelson Thornes), *Understanding Child Development* and *Equality in Early Childhood* (Hodder Arnold) and the *What Does it Mean to be ....?* series focusing on two, three, four and five year olds (Step Forward Publishing). Jennie writes for a range of early years magazines, but her most regular contributions are to Nursery World, Practical Pre-School and Practical Professional Child Care.

What does early literacy look like? In *A sofa full of talkers* Jennie examines the way young children acquire communication skills and how practitioners can manage the learning environment to help them do so effectively. She emphasises that children learn best in small groups where communication is personal and immediate. She stresses the importance of responding to the child's individual needs in a familiar, secure and supportive environment, and warns against the risk of diverting experienced individuals from appropriate practice, well grounded in knowledge of early child development.

We need to focus on early development. In recent years the level of concern in the UK has grown about older children who are unable to read and write, or who lack confidence in using under-developed literacy skills. It is an indictment of policy and practice when older children and young people, who have spent years in the education system, have not been enabled to crack the code for written language. It is also worrying when teenagers who have learned the technical details of how to read and write do not believe that these skills are relevant for their own, post-school life.

Nevertheless, concerned adults – parents, practitioners and policy-makers – need to prioritise their worrying and engage in some developmentally appropriate problem-finding and problem-solving. Otherwise, legitimate concerns about later literacy skills risk disrupting the crucial early foundations through children's confidence in their oral communication skills. There is reason to be concerned that at least some anxious adults have already imposed this consequence on young children – in some families, but also within some early years provision, where practitioners have lost their way.

This chapter is about really early language development, within the first three years of childhood. The communication skills of babies and very young children are exciting; they need to be respected in their own right. However, adult time and attention to these developments is the most appropriate, child-friendly and effective focus for literacy in really early childhood.

Speaking and listening skills come first

In recent years, there has been growing concern that an increasing number of young children struggle with speaking and listening skills. Local Speech and Language teams have reported an increase in referrals of under-fives who appear to be delayed in their language development. Anecdotal evidence has grown from primary school teams who describe children unable to express themselves clearly in words, hold a turn-taking conversation or listen carefully to other people. So what is happening?

1. There is no evidence of a significant increase in non-specific disabilities affecting the development of communication for the current very young generation. The explanation seems to be a restricted experience of social communication for some children.

2. An easy way out has been to blame families for letting their children watch many hours of television, instead of giving them personal attention. Some parents do hand over responsibility to a screen: television, computers or the myriad of electronic toys that are aggressively marketed as vital for 'getting children ready for school'.

3. Hard-pressed parents can find it tough to spend relaxed conversation and playtime with their children, and maybe also do not realise why these simple, family experiences need to be a top priority.

4. However, parent-blaming does not explain research and informal observation that seriously questions the quality of practice in some early years settings. A proportion of early years practitioners, and sometimes their leaders and advisors, have seriously lost their focus on what and how young children learn, and therefore on the most appropriate supportive adult role.

Writing in the bulletin of The Royal College of Speech and Language Therapists, Alison Weeks discusses developing an adult-child interaction approach in an early years centre because, 'staff said they were confident about planning and carrying out formal language activities, but they were less confident about facilitating language in everyday routines and play' (Weeks: 2004, p10). Research projects (for example Locke and Ginsborg, Dockrell et al.) have established that special programmes alone will not change nursery practice – in these instances for three to five year olds. In the contexts studied, special talking and listening times were not sustained, sometimes not even through the research phase, if a team's developmentally unwise priorities were left unchallenged. Some practitioners simply took the view that they had far too many activities to complete and targets to reach for them to 'waste time' listening to what children wished to say.

Across the UK a proportion of harassed practitioners have focussed on completion of pre-planned events, even down to adult-led 'communication activities'. Practitioners then pay less and less attention to what the babies and young children in front of them want to handle and share through non-verbal and verbal communication. The priority becomes an anxiety to tick off the written learning outcomes, allegedly achieved by getting even very young children to tolerate adult-dominated, often rather boring, activities. Such uncommunicative events also tend to occur in groups: a situation alien to the personal focus of young children, especially under threes. The largest group feasible for communication with young children is what I call a 'sofa-full'. Over-threes do not learn positive attitudes to communication, nor stretch their skills, in large groups where they have to wait to contribute and often cannot easily see the relevant book, puppet or other prop.

Some practitioners, and/or team leaders, do not value or understand the power of ordinary conversation, that oral communication is the non-negotiable underpinning of any proper literacy skills. Unfortunately, some early years practitioners have come to believe that 'just chatting' with children is pointless and time is far better spent on formal activities that 'get them ready for school'. Even down to the baby room, less well informed and/or pressurised practitioners, rush through impersonal care routines in order to create time for babies to sit in a circle and be questioned about adult-chosen items. Young toddlers (children between one and two years of age), who have yet to explore thoroughly that people and objects have words to name them, are drilled through 'shape of the week'. This activity is a genuine waste of adult and toddler time and is sometimes imposed on reluctant practitioners by a manager or nursery chain hierarchy who have a minimal grasp of child development.

The picture is not one of unrelenting gloom. Some parents continue to give relaxed time and generous communication to their young children. Some early years practitioners, across the different kinds of provision, understand the personal nature of early communication skills. But a proportion of adults have lost their way and it is necessary to consider what has disrupted personal and affectionate support for babies and very young children. Equally important, parents and practitioners who have children's best developmental interests in mind, need plenty of informative support to affirm that they are on the right track.

How does early language development unfold?

No single theory about early language development can explain completely how young children around the world learn to speak, often more than one language, within the years of early childhood. There are several, interrelated explanations about how young children are able to become enthusiastic communicators.

A consistent strand is that simple, personal approaches work best to support this exciting development. There is no need for adults to be taught complicated 'communication techniques'. Indeed, practical projects by speech and language teams and researchers aim to encourage people to use ordinary, everyday opportunities with individual babies and children. Unless children genuinely have a disability affecting communication, they do not need special coaching programmes, brought in by experts. Children need attentive and caring adults who behave like fellow human beings.

Babies are ready to tune into sound and language

Human babies are pre-programmed to be social, and their brains are well attuned to the sounds of human language. Within the first year of life a baby's brain becomes specialised for the sound patterns of the language(s) that can be heard in daily life. So babies are poised to learn language in the fullest sense; the early years are a crucial window of opportunity.

What practitioners should do:

- Offer personal contact; individual babies or toddlers learn from real

is for **Sheep**

people who share the warmth of eye contact, touch and words. Good habits need to continue for toddlers and young children: good communication happens at the eye level of a young child, so get down to their level.

- Make sure they have a baby or young child's attention before starting with words, a song or a visual game. Gain attention through gentle touch, eye contact, a smile and by saying their name at the beginning of the phrase, not at the end. Set a good example of courteous communication and also discover if currently this baby or toddler is more interested in something other than what you wish to say.

- Babies are very responsive to music and tuneful communication. Parents around the world sing to their babies and children, because very young children light up with the rhythm and repetition of simple songs. Toddlers soon choose to join in accompanying hand movements and may request a familiar song or nursery rhyme by demonstrating the relevant gestures.

- Recorded music works well, when pieces of music are chosen that vary in emotional tone. Notice what a baby or toddler seems to enjoy and play tunes, songs or pieces of classical music again. There is no evidence that specifically European classical music, Mozart or any other composer, boosts intelligence.

- Babies and young children need to be able to distinguish voices and what is said to them. Non-stop background music is not 'stimulating' for babies; it disrupts their concentration, because they have to filter out what has become 'sound wallpaper'. When speech and language therapists visit the homes of children whose language is delayed, their first request is often that parents switch off the television.

Communication is a personal business

Early language development is as much social and emotional as intellectual. Communication flourishes within personal, affectionate relationships: within family life and in a warm emotional atmosphere in out of home care.

Even babies are busy learning the social skills linked with sound-making. Babies younger than six months of age, who have experienced generous attention, can manage the simple turn taking of a very early 'conversation' with a familiar adult or child, like an older sibling. Young toddlers repeat gestures like pointing, when that form of communication has engaged an adult's attention. Older babies and young children repeat tuneful trills or deliberate sounds, like blowing raspberries, when adults or other children have responded with smiles or chortles.

Children, who have limited personal interaction, will most likely learn to talk, but their use of speech will be limited. Young children need to experience a wealth of child-focussed reasons why it is enjoyable to be a talker. They need to be motivated to use their speech out of personal choice, rather than following adult-initiated question-and-answer sessions – whether these are driven by a time-poor parent or misguided nursery group work. There is a strong, and worrying, parallel here with older children who can read, but choose not to be readers, unless an adult is pushing them.

What practitioners should do:

- Ensure there are plenty of relaxed times and places when babies can respond to you and a shared experience of play. Look and listen to the baby with his childminder in the Birth to Three Matters video section about 'A Skilful Communicator'. The baby is definitely joining in with the story read to the young girl and he adds his sound-comments.

- Babies and young children need a great deal of attention for their personal care routines and as they steadily move to share in their own care. Value the personal care and regular, domestic routines like mealtimes, as ideal times for the give-and-take of speaking and listening. The Birth to Three Matters cards for A Healthy Child offer detailed suggestions to talk with children about their choices and likes and the video shows a social mealtime, with an engaged and relaxed practitioner.

- Look at the lovely changing sequence towards the end of the Birth to Three Matters video. The practitioner shows respect for the toddler's own communication and attention to his personal needs. Listen to the voice-over for that sequence and you will hear reference to six of the component cards, including some on A Skilful Communicator. This sequence shows and tells very clearly that so much of this under-threes framework is 'delivered' to children through everyday experiences.

- Babies and young children must be enabled for develop personal relationships with their out of home carers. In any group setting, a key person system has to be operate that is truly personal, for children and parents. Group settings, or childminders for that matter, who are anxious that young children 'should not get too attached', will deprive young minds of vital emotional nutrition.

- Reflect on the messages for young children in your practice. If they were to ask themselves, 'Why should I speak', the confident reply needs to be, 'because my important people are interested in what I have to say'. A theoretical question from a young child of, 'Why should I listen' needs to

be answered, from their daily experiences by, 'because what people say is usually interesting to me, and because I get plenty of times when people listen to me in my turn.'

Sensible, communicative adults avoid plastic toys and electronic pads that claim to 'teach your child first words'. The most sophisticated internal circuitry does not know this toddler personally. Children learn meaningful language from real people, who are in a continuing personal relationship with them day by day. They do not learn language by being drilled by the disembodied voice of a total stranger powered by batteries.

Learning through imitation

Babies and young toddlers are keen to imitate the sounds and words that they hear. Direct copying partly explains how young children learn to speak, but is far from a complete explanation. Babies and toddlers happily produce some sounds and sequences of tuneful sounds that are original to them. They imitate recognisable words from the language they hear, but soon they are very creative about what they say. Toddlers use tone and emphasis to get maximum meaning out of single words, using a method of communication that they do not copy exactly from adults or older children.

Older toddlers and young two-year-olds combine words into their own phrases and short sentences. They produce samples of speech that they have not heard directly from the people around them. So they cannot be learning only from imitation; even very young children think about what they want to say and are busy making sense of their social world. However, imitation is the jumping off point: babies and toddlers need to hear plenty of spoken language that is meaningful for them.

What practitioners should do:

- Throughout the first year babies benefit from an adjusted kind of communication. They need adults to speak directly with them, but they tune in better when we use a more lively delivery than ordinary conversation. Babies respond with enthusiasm to an expressive style, with a 'musical' intonation and at a higher pitch than normal. Talk at a slow pace, with pauses, so that babies have the time to reply with sounds and gestures. Babies respond to a circling quality in adult speech; you need to repeat your message with slight variations.

- The delight for babies in infant-directed speech is that sometimes the adult, or older child, imitates the baby, following his or her lead. You set a good example of how conversation works: with speaking and pauses for paying attention through listening and looking.

- Children learn to listen by experiencing the respect of people paying attention to them. It is considerably less effective to focus on forever telling children to listen to you. It is also manifestly unfair, if you fail to provide a good example of a listener for them to imitate. By all means you can say something, or point out something of interest. But then pause and look expectant. Babies as young as young as 3-4 months 'say' something in that gap. Babies and toddlers imitate the conversational pattern; soon they make sounds, pause and look expectantly at you in their turn.

- Toddler powers of accurate imitation can be observed when they repeat phrases used by familiar people in the family or out-of-home care. They will reproduce, in the right context and with accurate tone, phrases like 'Herey'are', 'Whoops' and 'Lookadat'.

- Slightly older children, siblings or familiar children in out-of-home care, are often thrilled to 'teach' a younger child words like 'Ta' or 'Hello'. You need to keep a friendly ear and eye because some mischievous siblings find it amusing to drill younger ones in the wrong word!

- You use the power of imitation to help children. Toddlers' first words are very personal versions and you show respect by reacting to 'bir' as 'bird', since a toddler's eyes and pointing finger make the communication very clear. You then comment, 'Oh, yes, I can see the bird. There on the tree.' It works best to echo the young child's word, say it correctly and extend a little. Do not make the toddler repeat back 'bird'. He or she will hear and self-correct in their own good time.

- The same approach works very well when slightly older children use short phrases. You can extend a child's comment of, 'Mama work' to become, 'Yes, Mummy's gone to work now.' Logical grammatical mistakes like, 'I eated my dinner' are guided in the same way through gentle correction of, 'Yes, you ate up all your dinner – well done!'

Children flourish with encouragement

Babies and young children react positively to responsive adults and older children. Family life with friends, and out-of-home care provision, need to create time and space for children of different ages to play, chat together and enjoy shared routines like mealtimes. The birth to three guidance for Scotland focuses on the three Rs of relationships, responsive care and respect. This approach focuses strongly on communication and emotional security for very young children through the close relationship made with their out-of-home carer, supported through partnership with a child's family.

Babies repeat trills of sound that have provoked smiles and replies from an adult, or slightly older child, sibling or not. Speaking children extend their skills with the support of adults who look and sound genuinely interested in what young children want to share and say. Words come to link with non-verbal communication that has already been established. Older babies and toddlers have learned the power of pointing, by eye and finger, in order to bring an adult or another child into the communication exchange.

Toddlers' first words are an exciting development, but spoken language does not appear simply because they have passed a particular age barrier. Toddlers usually launch into real words, recognisable to people who know them well, somewhere within the second year of life. Spontaneous speech rests upon months of happy early communication - from single sound making, to trills of sound and generous use of eye and hand gesturing. Toddlers make the symbolic leap into words because they have been busy communicating from birth. They are already communicators; now they work at being talkers.

What practitioners should do:

- Children are motivated to use their communication skills because of rich experience of real people being interested in what they have to say. Personal encouragement cannot be delivered electronically. Ignore the claims on the packaging or company website, battery-driven toys and electronic so-called learning pads are not examples of social interaction. Being beeped or flashed at by a screen is not the same as smiles and cuddles from a real person.

- Babies and young children are alert to communication through body language. Show by your facial expression and tone that you genuinely enjoy spending time with individual children, with a book, a song, a conversation or just snuggling up together and watching the world go by. (The Birth to Three Matters cards use that actual phrase 'snuggling up' within A Competent Learner.)

- Young children have a sharp radar to judge whether an adult is genuinely interested. They pick up on a bored tone and 'I'm fed up' expression, regardless of the words.

- Children welcome your spoken communication that follows their lead. But they also appreciate the non-verbal encouragement that emerges from your willingness to wait. Hold onto good habits of using the power of the pause with young children who can express themselves in words. Avoid rushing to fill a silence, especially since young children require thinking time to organise what they want to say.

Thinking and communicating

Young children obviously think as well as speak and they are busy making sense of their world. Early evidence of very young thinking is demonstrated at the beginning of spoken language, even before. First words are exciting, because young children have made the big leap into the symbolism of language: that the same sound stands always for the same person or object. However, every young child's early words form a very personal list. There is no set 'first words' list that fits every child, because daily life and interests are different for individuals.

Toddlers' early, recognisable words relate to familiar people from the family or regular out of home childcare. Depending on toddlers' daily life, they may also go for words about loved cuddly toys, pets or liked food or drink. Many toddlers are fascinated by people smaller than themselves, so may say 'baby'. Items of clothing can be of direct interest, because a toddler can put them on or take them: like 'hat' or 'sock'. Words may be linked to interesting items that a young child sees, especially ones that move like 'lorry' or do something intriguing like 'bubbles'. Toddlers often learn some words for pictures or characters in a favourite book, because books are already part of a happy, personal time in their family or nursery.

What practitioners should do:

- Ensure that what you say to young children connects easily and obviously to what is currently in front of both of you. Babies and very young toddlers relate to real objects and people. Older toddlers have made the move into understanding that a picture of a banana is also called by the same word, although you cannot eat a picture. Soon they make the next connection into small world figures: that this tiny item is also a chair, although you cannot sit on it.

- Young children need to understand words before they say them. They need to grasp how your words are connected with something meaningful - otherwise words are just sounds. Young children need plenty of relaxed opportunities to hear words in their relevant context before they are likely to say the word spontaneously. The Birth to Three Matters cards have plenty of encouragement to promote adult comments rather than cross-questioning – see for example the Competent Learner cards.

- Young children generally develop their understanding of words before they say them. They will show that they grasp 'doll', because they relish a spotting game with, 'Where's the doll?' and 'Where's your nose?' before they use either word themselves. Playful exchanges show you, and parents, that young toddlers understand a range of words in a context that makes sense to them.

 is for **Sheep**

- Be close to very young children and be ready to link your words with what interests them. Name the objects that toddlers touch and want to play with – 'you've got the ball'. 'where's your shoe? There it is!'. Affirm the names of familiar people, that children can see: 'Here's Sasha, come to play with you' or 'I can see your Daddy'.

- Follow the children's lead and avoid any temptation to drill them to learn an adult-generated list of words. If the atmosphere is friendly, then toddlers may cooperate, but they have not grasped genuine meaning.

- Respond to young children's creative use of single words and show you understand their full communication. A questioning tone from a toddler in 'Teddy?', guides you to say, 'Have you lost Teddy? Let's find Teddy.' A crooning sound to 'Teddy' invites you to comment, 'We found Teddy. You're cuddling your Teddy now.'

- Toddlers and young children need books as a personal time, not a large group, and ideally as often as possible when children themselves seize a favourite book and wave it at you to be enjoyed and read. Children as young as 16 months then have favourite books, have started to understand how books and stories work and soon they echo or tell parts of familiar stories.

Different kinds of words

Apart from little phrases they imitate from you, toddlers' earliest spoken language includes words to name people and things (grammatically these are the nouns). Once they have words to name, then you will hear toddlers use words that denote actions (these are the verbs). Action, or doing words, are again personal to a young child, since they are motivated to use words that make sense in their daily life. A toddler who has regular trips to the pool will start to use 'swim' or 'swimming'. Toddlers may use variations of jump, eat, drink, get-it or get-up, sing, dance and any other action words that stand for what this child does, with you and their friends. Action words also function as a request to you: that toddlers want you to jump in the air, or to lift them so they can jump.

Once young children have plenty of naming and action words in their spontaneous spoken vocabulary, they will start to use descriptive words in a meaningful way. But once again, the actual words will depend on this young child's interests. Children who experience nice food may use 'tasty' or 'crunchy'. Keen outdoors players may have 'deep' for their hole, 'high' for the clambering frame or 'wet' for the puddle. None of these ideas words can exist without a naming or action words. The hole is deep; children climb high up the frame. Grammatically these descriptive words are either adjectives - that add meaning to the nouns- or adverbs - that add further meaning to the verbs.

What practitioners should do:

- Watch and listen to young children's interests and drop appropriate ideas words into the conversation, when they will be meaningful. Children do not learn their colours by being drilled in 'colour of the week'. Sensible adults comment on colour when it is relevant: 'Come and see our lovely yellow sunflowers' or 'I like your red boots – very elegant!'

- Abstract ideas are learned through direct experiences – hands-on, eyes-on, feet-on, ears-on. Listen to what two-year-olds say, as well as watch what they do. You will realise that these very young children have grasped a range of concepts. Some of them may well have tuned into colour, but not all. Young children, currently uninterested in colours, may have a subtle grasp of light and dark, heavy or speed. There is no sound developmental reason to support the priority now given within early years practice to colour and shape.

- Throw out the plastic toys that claim to teach very young children colour, shape, numbers, letters – everything that can be jammed onto the surface or programmed into the stranger's voice. Young children cannot distinguish any of these ideas from the visual and sound jumble. Additionally some of these 'learning' resources are targeted at babies and very young toddlers who have yet to fathom that people and objects have names.

Messages that mislead

Early years practitioners and parents experience ill-informed messages that suggest 'earlier must be better' on the formal literacy front. Look around any large toy store and notice how many toys have letters and numbers stuck to the plastic or cloth surface. Read what is written on the packaging, look at the websites of the most prominent companies.

This level of abstraction is aggressively promoted by some companies, right down to the baby year. So-called early learning kits and electronic consoles push the advisability of starting abstract, written symbols with babies and toddlers who have not yet gained skills in spoken language. Regrettably some books and magazine articles, even in publications for early years practitioners, promote activities for very young children that clutter daily life with written, single letters and numbers. Much of this headlong rush is justified as a necessary 'getting them ready for school', even in some cases as supported by research into brain development. Any written letters, words or numbers should communicate a

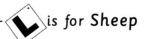
is for **Sheep**

message, whether they are on a book, picture or play resource. If letters or numbers are saying nothing to adults or older children, then they are certainly empty of meaning for younger children.

It is not entirely surprising that some parents ask early years practitioners 'when is she going to read' or dismiss a child's careful emergent writing as 'just scribble'. Some deeply unwise practice, even with toddlers and two-year-olds, then gets established with the excuse of, 'but it's what the parents want'. Practitioners in any group settings, and childminders working in their own home, need to be clear about why it is such poor practice to impose flash cards on toddlers or make two-year-olds trace round letters. Early years professionalism needs to be strong, so that a parent's query, or a challenge from anyone else, is met with, 'I'm so glad you asked. We are/I am passionate about early literacy. I/we would be delighted to show you how we build firm foundations through....'

Really early literacy looks like this!

Firm foundations for reading and writing are created by developmentally appropriate adult behaviour and flexible planning within the early years. Older children will not be poised to decode written language unless they are confident and competent in their spoken language(s). Really early literacy, starting properly with the under-threes means all of the following.

Talkers are doing early literacy

Young children build firm foundations, when they are given time to learn and practise their skills of spoken communication. Keen talkers, even under-threes, are able to put their thoughts into words. You can hear the sounds of their thinking represented by their spoken language. Writing is not only about the technicalities of handwriting. School age children need to be able to talk out and plan what they want to write.

Keen talkers have also, even by three years of age, shifted into different uses of language and these functions will, in time, be reflected in their communication through writing. Young three-year-olds can use their spoken language to inform and explain, to tell about an event in the recent past, to remind adults about 'what you said we'd do today'. All these uses of language, and more that will now develop, build a firm foundation that will support later reasons 'why we might want to write something down.'

Love of books is early literacy

Young children need to be enthused by books: story books and picture books that tell and show about the world. Young children start to look like readers and they build motivation for the tough task ahead of actually learning to read. They have learned that books are worthwhile for them, children have informed opinions about the plots and characters they have encountered and believe that some books tell you interesting information.

Pretend narratives are early literacy

Happy experience of stories in book form can link together with the developing pretend play of young children. Imaginative play starts within the second year of life and two-year-olds steadily extend their sequences of pretend, before they launch into the complex role play you can observe with three- and four-year-olds. Young children who enjoy pretend play are busy creating their own narratives. This experience of story telling equips them with more reasons to want to write when they are ready.

Singing and rhyming is early literacy

Young children who enjoy singing and rhymes will have practised, in a most enjoyable way, the sounds of their own language(s). English, in particular, is a very difficult, non-regular language. The written form is very tough to learn because every spelling rule, and grammar, has exceptions. So children need plenty of non-pressurised experiences that encourage them to play around with the sounds of spoken English.

Painting and drawing is early literacy

Young children, who have had generous supplies of stationery for drawing and painting, make the shift into meaningful mark making. Look at the baby painting with his hands in the Birth to Three Matters video. At this very young age, he shows powers of concentration and is already learning how to make deliberate marks. Young children learn the motivation to want to make marks and practise the physical skills and co-ordination that will thoroughly support them well, when they are ready to learn to write. Adults who set a good example of using writing for practical reasons will have contributed to children's sense of purpose about writing – why people do it, what writing can do for us. Young children are poised to become writers for their own, personal reasons, not because adults seem to be extremely keen on this skill.

References

Attenborough, Liz and Fahey, Rachel (2005) <u>Why do many young children lack basic language skills?</u> Discussion paper for National Literacy Trust *(see www.talktoyourbaby.org.uk)*

Cousins, Jacqui (2003) <u>Listening to four year olds: how they can help us plan their education and care</u>. London, National Children's Bureau

Dockrell, Julie, Stuart, Morag and King, Diane <u>Talking Time: supporting effective practice in preschool provision</u> *(see www.literacytrust.org.uk/talktoyourbaby/*

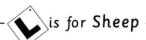 is for Sheep

talkingtimeproject.pdf)

Early Childhood Unit, <u>Listening as a way of life</u> (set of leaflets) *(contact www.earlychildhood.org.uk)*

Edwards, Anna Gillespie (2002) <u>Relationships and Learning: caring for children from birth to three</u>. London, National Children's Bureau

Healy, Jane (2004) <u>Your Child's Growing Mind: brain development and learning from birth to adolescence</u>. New York, Broadway

Karmiloff-Smith, Annette (1996) <u>Baby it's You: a unique insight into the first three years of the developing baby</u>. London, Ebury Press

Learning and Teaching Scotland (2005) <u>Birth to Three: supporting our youngest children</u>. *(see www.ltscotland.org.uk/earlyyears/birthtothree)*

Lindon, Jennie (2005) <u>Understanding Child Development: linking theory and practice</u>. London, Hodder Arnold

Lindon, Jennie; Kelman, Kevin and Sharp, Alice (2006, second edition) <u>Play and Learning for the Under Threes</u>. London, TSL Education

Lindon, Jennie (2006) <u>What Does it Mean to be Two? a practical guide to child development</u>. Leamington Spa, Step Forward Publishing

Locke, Ann and Ginsborg, Jane (2003) <u>Spoken Language in the Early Years: the cognitive and linguistic development of three- to five-year-old children from socio-economically deprived backgrounds</u>. *Educational and Child Psychology, volume 20 (4) 68-79*

Murray, Lynne and Andrews, Liz (2000) <u>The Social Baby</u>. Richmond, The Children's Project

SureStart (2002) <u>Birth to Three Matters: a framework to support children in their earliest years</u>. London, DfES

Weeks, Alison (2004) <u>Responsive Interaction</u>. *Royal College of Speech and Language Therapists (RCSPLT) Bulletin,* June

L is for Sheep

Penny Tassoni
Tuning in

Penny Tassoni is an education consultant, author and trainer, who trained and worked as an early years and primary school teacher before becoming a college lecturer. She specialises in the whole spectrum of early learning and play.

Penny has written nineteen books, including the best selling 'Planning Play and the Early Years' (Heinemann, 2005). She also writes for several magazines, including features for parents. Penny is an experienced trainer and her workshops feature at the Primary and Early Years exhibitions in both London and Manchester, as well as in the professional development programmes of many local authorities. In addition to training, Penny works as a reviser for CACHE, the awarding body for childcare, education and playwork qualifications in the U.K. She has worked as a consultant and key note speaker in Istanbul and Japan. Penny is Chair of A2P, a charity whose aim is to educate teenagers about the realities of having a baby.

In *Tuning in* Penny sets early reading firmly in the context of child development. She explores the ways in which children learn to recognise sounds and construct words, and the vital role of adults in supporting these processes. Penny argues that there is no point spending time on phonics until children have mastered these key processes of tuning in. There is additional help and guidance for helping children for whom English is a second language, and those with learning difficulties.

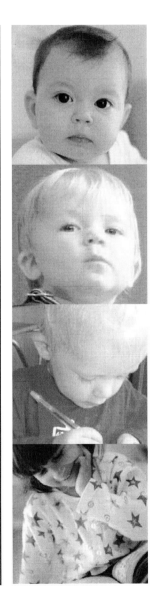

In the seemingly endless debate about reading methods, there is concensus that children need good speaking and listening skills in order to get off to a good start. The importance of speaking and listening is particularly relevant when it comes to using phonics with children, as the emphasis on auditory discrimination requires them to be able to hear sounds in words. This chapter looks at how this process begins in early childhood and focuses on the needs of children who may require additional support.

The development of speaking and listening skills requires fuller and more intensive attention to make sure that children acquire a good stock of words, learn to listen attentively, and speak clearly and confidently. These skills are the foundations of phonic work, for example, in building phonemic awareness. Moreover, they are prime communication skills, hugely important in their own right and central to children's intellectual, social and emotional development. (Rose: 2005)

The starting point for hearing the sounds in words begins early in a child's life. It actually starts before birth as the unborn baby is already reacting to sounds and music from around 26 weeks. Research has shown that unborn babies can actually remember after birth certain significant sounds that they were exposed to in the final trimester of the mother's pregnancy. This means that in the first few days after being born most babies quickly recognise not only the smell of their mothers, but also their voices. Thus the process of tuning into language has already begun.

It is a steady process which takes several months and is usually referred to as the pre-linguistic phase. It is a vital stage as babies begin to break into the code of sounds and learn how these sounds act as symbols. This phase also teaches babies some of the basic, but nonetheless essential skills of how to communicate with others. Eye contact, turn taking and facial expression of adults are all mirrored by the baby and amazingly, by the age of nine or ten months, most babies are able to understand the meaning of a few words. Interestingly, at around this time babies' vocalisations increasingly mirror the sounds that will be required in the language that they are being exposed to. In a phase known as linguistic contraction, sounds that are not required become redundant, and from this point on it is possible to differentiate between babies who are learning different languages.

First words

While the pre-linguistic phase is marked by the baby's need to tune into the language, the linguistic phase is marked by the emergence of words. At around 12 or 13 months, most babies will produce their first words. Ironically, these can be missed at first because they are often popped in alongside strings of babbling. But

sooner or later, the adult does notice and responds quickly. A child's first words are almost always the ones that are immediately useful, and usually refer to objects, people and food! The notable exception to this is the word 'no', which toddlers soon find out can be used to communicate their rejection of further food, drink or being put down for a nap. By two years, toddlers are beginning to acquire words rapidly and are often combining them to make mini-sentences, known as 'telegraphese'. By three years, most children's speech is becoming clearer and fluent, although because of the development of the tongue, jaw and teeth, speech is not fully mature until around six years old (see table below). This has some implications for phonic teaching, as it means that children may not always be able to reproduce the sounds that they are meant to be recognising and learning.

$2\frac{1}{2}$ years	p,b,m,n	Consonants are produced by the lips
3 years	h,w,t,d	By this age children's speech should be mostly intelligible
$3\frac{1}{2}$ years	g,k,y	
4 years+	f,sh,ch,bl,fl,sl,sn, st,kr,gr,sm,str	Consonant blends begin at around four years, but the full range is not acquired until 7 or so years.
5 years+	l,z,v,s,r	
7 years	'th' as in thumb	Up until this age, children are often using 'w' instead of 'r' in words such as rabbit.

Typical sequence of the production of sounds in Australian English, based upon Kilminster and Laird (1978)

How adults help babies to tune into sounds

While babies seem to be primed to learn language at birth, this process is hugely dependent on the role of the adult. Fortunately, adults caring for babies seem also to be primed to respond to the baby's linguistic needs! It is worth examining the actions of adults in helping children to tune into language as there are lessons here for helping children to read.

Adults make language learning a fun and emotionally warm experience

If you ever watch a parent with their baby, you will see immediately that there is much playfulness during the interaction. The adult smiles, laughs and tries to engage with the child. There is also a significant amount of warmth towards the child. The baby quickly learns that language learning is fun and positive. This in turn encourages the baby and prompts increasing vocalisations.

Adults make language learning meaningful for the child

If we record the content of an adult's interaction with a child, we will find that the adult aims to make it meaningful for the child. Words are repeated and phrases are simplified so that the child can pick out the key words. The pitch of the voice is higher and more expressive than if the adult were talking to another adult. Even the facial expression is magnified, with eye brows raised and large smiles. No wonder that language learning is so appealing for the baby.

Interactions are also very child centred. Language is based around what the baby is doing and what the adult knows the baby enjoys doing. Interactions are very much in the 'here and now' rather than in the abstract. A running commentary style is used to talk about what the baby is doing, be that feeding, crying or playing peep-po. Language is also made meaningful by drawing the child's attention to objects of interest and people in the child's immediate environment. This is usually done by taking the baby over to the object or person and by the adult pointing so that the meaning of the word is clear. Interestingly, babies quickly catch on to the usefulness of pointing, and we can see them replicate this as a tactic to draw the adult's attention to something that they want. Pointing alongside vocalisations remains a major tool in a child's communication kit for a couple of years afterwards.

Adults make the experience sensory

We also find that adults are usually good at combining language learning with sensory experiences in babies' first years. Bath time is conducted with a running commentary, as is feeding and even nappy changing. Babies are also often held and played with during language interactions. This makes the language learning more effective as we know that sensory experiences are powerful ones for young children and can assist memory. Babies are often held during interactions with adults, and again this is a sensory pleasure that generates feelings of warmth and security and encourages the baby to concentrate on the language.

Adults spend time drawing children's attention to sounds and reinforce learning

While few parents caring for their child would say that they have a structured programme for language learning the reality is that, in a natural way, parents do spend time reinforcing sounds and language. They do this through playing rhyme games with their children, and by singing and repeating phrases and words during

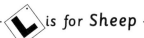

the everyday care routines. Adults also seem programmed to rock and jog babies in time to songs and rhymes. Imagine what *Humpty Dumpty* would be like if the adult didn't put the child on the knee and jog him in time to the words. Hearing the beat and the sounds by using rhymes and songs helps strengthen the child's interest in tuning in. Again, this is soon reflected in the quality of babies' babbling. Babbling changes form and structure in response to babies' awareness of the pattern and intonation of the language to which they are being exposed. Indeed there is a phase in language learning during which children have literally learnt the tunes, but have not quite got the words!

Adults respond to the child's pace

Most babies' language learning follows a sequence, and adults are usually instinctively good at responding to the baby's pace of progress. Interactions are based on the child's interests and previous knowledge. The adult switches to another topic, object or game if the baby begins to lose interest. In the same way the adult continues if the child is appearing interested and will naturally extend the language. Adults seem to be good at being flexible in their approach and working out what stimulates the child.

Amazingly, adults also seem to be good at knowing when to expect more of their child. Linguists have noticed that many parents increase the complexity of their sentences fairly naturally. Adults are also good at interpreting the baby's early attempts at words and communication, and responding with a smile, a cuddle or by offering the baby a toy. Immediate action such as this reinforces for the child that language learning does pay dividends.

Tuning in and phonics

The process of tuning into the sounds of English is a pre-requisite for learning phonics. Children have to be able to hear the sounds in words and to be able to relate them to symbols in order to master a phonetic approach to reading. There are, however, some groups of children who may need additional support and time as they may not have yet reached the stage of development where they are able to recognise and discriminate the sounds of English.

Children who have not been exposed to English in their earliest years

The United Kingdom has become a culturally rich society with a range of diverse linguistic elements. This has meant that in many schools there are children who are speakers of a language other than English, either as their primary means of communication or as an additional tongue. In some cases, children may be mastering three languages, or even more. The first question before the teaching of phonics to these children can begin is whether or not they are sufficiently able to recognise and pick out the sounds of the English language. The second question is whether they have sufficient vocabulary for the language to have meaning for them once they are able to read it.

Helping children acquire English from scratch!

It is not unusual for pre-school settings and schools to work with children who are literally learning English from scratch. Guidance on supporting these children can be patchy, but actually the principles for helping them are not unlike those described above when adults are with babies. Where children have already mastered a home language, they can be very quick to tune into English, provided that support and encouragement are provided early on. Hoping that children will just pick it up is not enough, and by placing demands on children which they are not yet equipped to meet it can make them feel emotionally insecure. A little intense effort means that children settle in more quickly and acquire English more easily.

Here are some suggestions and ideas to help practitioners enable children to tune into the sounds of English:

- Use a key person system. Make sure that the child spends sufficient time with one designated adult. In pre-school settings this should be the key person. This is essential, as it means that children have one emotionally responsive adult to whom they can turn. Having one 'special' adult who focuses on the child speeds up the tuning in process. It is much harder to become familiar with the sounds of a language if the accents, intonation, voice pitch and even facial expression keep changing.

- Be expressive. While baby talk is not appropriate, the skills of using facial expression and exaggeration are. Point to objects, smile and focus on the key words in a sentence. Repeat a word while pointing.

- Don't worry if children are quiet at first. Tuning in takes a little time and there is a stage where children, like babies, have obviously acquired the meaning of a few key words but are not yet ready to say them. Pressurising children into saying things before they are ready can actually delay their speech.

- Focus on the here and now. Point to objects and people, and use photos and books so that children can work out the subject of the conversation. Remember that children will learn first the words that have the most meaning for them. Work out what they enjoy doing and looking at, and use this as a basis.

- Create language routines. If a phrase is repeated several times a day in predicable situations, children will quickly pick it up. In the same way, children can be quick to pick up songs and rhymes (see traditional rhymes below).

- Find out about home language use. It is important to find out about home language and its use. Occasionally, a child who is not communicative in English despite the best efforts of adults may in fact not be speaking much of their home language either. Finding out from parents how much the child speaks at home is therefore useful. Where parents are using more than one language at home - e.g. a mix of Portugese, English and Turkish - it is also important to find out who is using what and when. Adults who are used to communicating in more than one language will often switch effortlessly from one language to another. This language hopping can be confusing to young children because it prevents them from working out the grammatical rules of the language. Not surprisingly, this will delay their linguistic development and is one reason why some children either fail to talk or mix their languages. A rule for very young children that is usually effective is one person, one language. Taking an earlier example, this would mean that a mother wanting her child to learn Turkish would only address her child in Turkish, but the father would address the child in Portuguese. If the language of communication between the couple was English, they would speak to each other in English, but they would always address the child in their respective languages. In this way language use for the child becomes predictable and he is able to tune into each language and use it effectively.

Ways of helping children to tune in

There are several ways of drawing children's attention to sounds; some of them are described briefly below. Many are considered good practice and are regularly employed in the best settings, but where children may have missed out on the 'tuning in' stage of development, they need particular emphasis.

Listening out for sounds

Games that encourage children to listen out for particular sounds are useful. Such games can help children's auditory discrimination and can be based on the sounds in English as well as other sounds such as a shaker. A simple game is to have two people making different sounds – one might repeatedly being saying the 'ch' sound whilst the other might be saying 'sh'. The children have to work out who is saying the 'ch'. The game can also be played with musical instruments such as shakers. One child is out of sight and from time to time shakes a shaker. Another child is making a distracting sound with a drum. The other children have to listen out for the shaker.

When these type of games are played in groups, it is worth watching the reactions of children. Notice children who are slower to react or copy others.

Traditional nursery rhymes

Some of the strongest 'English' sounds can be found in traditional nursery rhymes. The powerful nature of these rhymes is why they have survived for hundreds of years and in times where the majority of the population was illiterate. The use of rhymes with babies and young children is a feature of parenting in many languages. Rhymes provide babies and young children with a sense of beat, rhythm, but they also draw children's attention to key sounds. A favourite of mine is *Diddle, Diddle Dumpling, My Son John*. If you know this rhyme and say it aloud, you will hear a clear meter, but also some strong initial and final sounds. In addition there are some key blends such as 'ing' and 'on'. All children benefit from having a good repertoire of the traditional rhymes, but children who are learning English and have not 'tuned' in during their first years will particularly benefit. The strength of the rhymes helps children to pick them up quickly and they are often able to join in, even though they may not be speaking fluently. Interestingly, the traditional rhymes also tidy up adult diction, compelling the speaker to pronounce the proper endings of words which in everyday speech they drop. This draws children's attention to some of the otherwise hidden sounds.

More recent rhymes have superceded some of the traditional ones, such as *The Wheels on the Bus* and *Five Fat Sausages*. This is partly in response to anxieties about the language and underlying messages of some of the traditional rhymes. While children do enjoy the modern rhymes and songs, the question which needs to be asked is whether these alone will help the children who really need it tune into English. There is an argument that the benefits of traditional rhymes in helping otherwise disadvantaged children outweigh misgivings over content. Having said that, it would still be prudent to avoid overtly negative rhymes such as *What are Little Boys Made Of?*

Using alliteration

Alliteration – the repetition of consonants – is fun for children. It is another way of drawing attention to sounds, usually the initial ones. Some tongue twisters, such as *Peter picked a peck of pickled peppers* can be wonderfully useful in helping children's diction. More simply, we can also look for ways of alliterating a child's name. 'Hurry, Harry' 'Smiley Sam'. This personalisation helps to make language fun and again supports the development of auditory discrimination. Similarly, some situations lend themselves to alliteration – magic mealtimes, sumptious snacktime.

Helping children who have problems

Children with some hearing loss

A further group of children who may not have tuned into English are those with a hearing loss. If phonics is to be the predominant way in which reading is to be taught, it is essential to be aware of these children's needs and also to be vigilant in watching for children who may have a yet unidentified hearing problem.

Helping children with identified hearing loss

Where a child has an identified hearing loss, it is important to talk to parents to find out when the loss was detected and its extent. Significant hearing loss, usually of a sensorineural nature is often picked up during the first year of a child's life. Parents may notice that the child appears unresponsive to sounds or is withdrawn. Babies who are not hearing are not likely to vocalise as much as other children and babbling does not progress to be tuneful and reflective of the speech patterns in the language to which they are being exposed. Whilst with identified hearing loss may be progressing well with their speech and language, it is still important to work in a focused way to help them 'tune' into the sounds in words. It is also important to recognise that hearing aids do help children enormously, but they are not perfect and children can still be missing out.

Signs of hearing loss

Many children can have hearing loss of a fluctuating nature. This is usually the result of fluid build up in the Eustacian tube, especially in the winter months. Children who are prone to this type of hearing loss are not always identified. Their apparent lack of attention, behaviour or lack of responsiveness is sometimes attributed to their 'character'. The fluctuation in their levels of hearing also means that even if hearing loss is suspected, they may come back with an all clear result!

Children with speech delay

There are many reasons why some children's speech may be slow to develop. Hearing loss, environmental conditions and learning difficulties are common factors. Whatever the underlying reason, children's speech needs to be sufficiently developed for them to make the composite sounds of English. Listening out to children's speech and being aware of atypical immaturities is therefore essential. Early referral to speech and language services can help reduce the overall impact on a child's development.

Making words count

Finally, it is also worth remembering that some children, although quite talkative and sounding apparently fluent, may not have developed some areas of vocabulary. This can be particularly true of children who have more than one language. Generally, vocabulary is acquired in context. Children who are not hearing English at home may be missing some of the words found in this context: e.g. 'tray', 'sieve' or 'armchair'. In the same way, children may have learnt some 'generic' words that are used to generalise, such as 'cars' or 'shoes', but may not have some of the more specific naming words such as 'truck' 'tractor', 'slippers' and 'lace ups'. Being aware of the need to build detailed vocabulary can prevent situations where children are reading words that have little meaning for them.

The key task for the practitioner in helping children develop sensitivity to and awareness of the sounds of language, is to put herself in the position of each individual child. It is important to ask questions such as 'What is helping this child tune into English, or what is inhibiting them from doing so?' By looking at factors such as the stage of language development, the home environment, individual needs and the stimulus and support available in the setting we can go a long way towards ensuring that all children get a fair start in the long journey towards successful listening, speaking, reading and writing.

Reference
Porter, Louise (2002) Educating Young Children with Special Needs. London, Paul Chapman

L is for *Sheep*

Part 2

The Phonics Debate

How have we got where we are?

The attention currently given to phonics is not new. Teachers, researchers and the education community have been talking about the place and development of phonological awareness in young children for a long time. The debate has become a political football regularly in the past, with opposing sides lining up in Parliament to state the case for different methods of teaching children to read and to argue whether the preferred method of the time should become enshrined in educational law. Some of the predecessors to the current debate are outlined below.

- In 1949 a bill to introduce simplified spelling in all schools missed by three votes becoming government policy. A Spelling Reform Bill was tabled again in 1953, but was withdrawn after the second reading when the government of the day agreed to fund research into reading.

- In the 1960s the Initial Teaching Alphabet (which promised to help early readers by removing spelling anomalies from the English language) was adopted in schools in Oldham and several other local authorities, before dying away when longer term research indicated no lasting benefit after transition to orthodox spelling.

- Reading schemes employing phonic methods, such as the Gay Way series, employed a simple, structured vocabulary for graded reading books, and these were used widely until very recently, sometimes alongside 'look and say' and 'whole language' books.

- In 1985, Liz Waterland's book *Read With Me* described an 'apprenticeship' approach to reading, where children were encouraged to become apprentices to people who could already read. At the time of writing, Waterland's book is still in print, and the methods it described have been adopted by many teachers and schools, with reports of huge success for many children;

- Research and writing by experts including Frank Smith, Usha Goswami, Marian Whitehead, Nigel Hall and many others, both nationally and internationally, continue to underpin and expand good practice in the beginning stages of reading. These include providing a wide and rich language experience for young children, leaving formal programmes until the children's brains and bodies are ready, and setting early reading in a curriculum rich in movement, rhyme, talk and music.

- In the USA, one piece of research appeared to find that a government supported programme of phonic teaching was ineffective and poor value for money, another lauded its success, and a third found that the positive effect of phonic teaching could be tripled when combined with a rich language approach. Phonics is indubitably part of the reading repertoire, but it would seem that the case for treating phonics as the sole or main tool for reading is yet to be proved.

- The National Curriculum, which made 'hear and say initial and final sounds in words and short vowel sounds within words,' and 'link sounds and letters' a requirement for the end of the Foundation Stage, and 'teach phonemic awareness and phonic knowledge as a reading strategy' a requirement for children in key Stage 1, set the teaching and learning of reading in a broad, language rich environment, where teachers are expected to use their professional judgement in matching their teaching strategies to children's needs.

- The National Literacy Strategy (1998) gave detailed, non statutory guidance to all schools and reception settings on the teaching of reading through a wide range of skills and methods (this became known as the 'searchlight' method). In the early stages of implementation, guidance covered phonological awareness, phonics and spelling within Word Work, taught as a discrete part of the literacy hour.

- Later guidance and materials issued by the Literacy Strategy (NLNS) and the Standards Unit, together with associated training, included Progression in Phonics and Playing With Sounds, the latter being the focus for much useful work in schools, settings and local authorities. It was unfortunate that these materials, intended for practitioners in the Foundation Stage, were only made available to practitioners outside the maintained sectors in a few enlightened local authorities where training opportunities were truly multi-disciplinary.

- More recently, the discussions have become heated again when practice and subsequent research into a programme of Synthetic Phonics implemented in Clackmannanshire claimed really astonishing gains in reading ability after a relatively short period of implementation, and an evaluation which contained several shortcomings.

- A Parliamentary Review of Reading has been established to take evidence on the teaching of Reading in the UK and in other countries.

- In 2005 Jim Rose, for Director of Inspections for OFSTED, was commissioned to conduct an independent review of the teaching of early reading. This report, published in March 2006, is likely to have a

 is for Sheep

significant effect on government policy and advice to teachers and practitioners working in the Foundation Stage and Key Stage 1. Findings and recommendations are being taken into account by the Primary Strategy when reviewing the Literacy Strategy and by the working parties constructing the guidance for the Early Years Foundation Stage.

In the next section, four more contributors – Linda Pound, Margaret Edgington, Janet Moyles and Janet Evans – explore existing good practice for very young children in acquiring readiness for a formal phonic programme. Each highlights areas and experiences of particular importance. These thoughts and opinions are a second strand in supporting the professional judgement of teachers and practitioners on the teaching of reading and the current debate on the use of phonics.

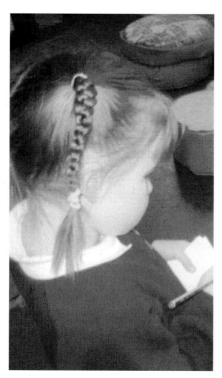

L is for Sheep

Linda Pound
Sounds good to me!

Linda Pound has spent a lifetime working with young children and their families. She was the deputy head of an infants' school where she established and ran a large nursery unit. Subsequently she became head of a maintained inner-city nursery school. For almost ten years she was the early years inspector for a local education authority in a London borough.

Linda has worked at three universities, most recently as academic leader for early childhood programmes at London Metropolitan University. The largest by far of the programmes offered there was a part-time degree course for experienced early years practitioners. This experience underlined for her the power of practical experience when strengthened by theoretical insight – giving practitioners the confidence to speak up for children.

Currently Linda works as a freelance consultant, providing training both in the UK and overseas and advising practitioners in a wide variety of settings. Linda has written a number of books, including 'How Children Learn: From Montessori to Vygotsky - Educational Theories and Approaches Made Easy' (Step Forward Publishing, 2005) and 'Supporting Musical Development in the Early Years' (Open University Press, 2002).

In *Sounds good to me!* Linda considers the part played by music, rhyme and dance as tools for thinking, and explores the role of sound in helping children to develop sensitivity to and awareness of phonics.

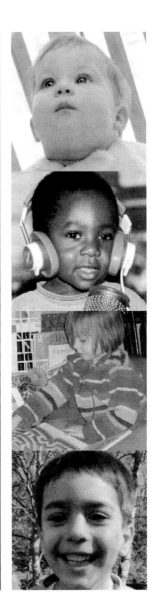

It is beyond dispute that in order to read children need phonic knowledge. However in teaching phonics we have to take account of other factors that characterise young children's learning, if the learning and teaching of phonics is to be successful in creating enthusiastic readers. The learning needs to be playful, to build on what children know and to draw on both child-initiated and adult-directed strategies. Phonics teaching all too often relies heavily on adult-led direct teaching – with insufficient opportunity for the practice and fun that playful strategies allow. Moreover a detailed programme of structured sessions risks overlooking or underestimating the knowledge and understanding that children already have.

It is equally beyond dispute that phonic knowledge, although essential, is not sufficient to becoming a reader. Children try to make sense of the world of print by searching for familiar words and patterns of letters. They also – in common with adult, experienced readers – draw on their knowledge of story, of everyday language and of book language in their search for sense. In English, as in many other languages, phonic knowledge must be employed in conjunction with experience of what the text might possibly say. For example, the emergent reader must learn that 'ough' says 'aw' works phonetically in bought and fought, but not in cough, bough or rough. Dealing with the complications of deciding how to arrive at the correct phonic response to this grapheme depends on memorisation and our linguistic experience of knowing what to expect.

The importance of musical elements

Music is common to all cultures. In every society music has a number of important roles or functions – enjoyment, mood creation, ceremony, commerce and so on. Virtually everyone responds to music, even some with profound hearing loss. Tests and observations show that very young babies react to music, as do many animals. The fact that music is universal indicates that it has an important biological and evolutionary part to play in human learning and development. It seems that human brains in particular are 'hard wired' to respond powerfully to music.

Music supports the development of social learning and interaction in two main ways. Firstly, it is widely used to create or reflect mood or atmosphere. The music played at funerals, parties, assemblies and even the accompaniment of 'muzak' when shopping are all everyday examples of music creating a shared mood. Secondly, music contributes to group cohesion, giving people a sense of belonging. Football songs, religious music and playground chants are common examples of the ways in which music binds groups together by creating cohesion and a common sense of belonging. Early childhood practitioners are very well

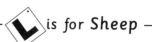
is for Sheep

aware of this, and experienced educators know how effective music is in bringing together a group of children to simply begin singing a favourite song. Within a very short space of time everyone will be joining in with enthusiasm.

Memory is aided and triggered by music. This occurs in very general ways. We can all conjure up a wealth of memories just from hearing a few bars of a familiar piece or a favourite song. We may remember a place where we have heard it, what we were wearing or doing when we heard it and who else was present; it may even conjure recollections of the mood or emotions we were experiencing at the time. We know the words (or some of them) to literally thousands of songs, which we seem to have learnt without any effort. Adults in middle and old age can often recall with remarkable accuracy the words of hymns they sang in school assembly many years before and have not sung since.

This link between song and memory is widely exploited in education. The alphabet song is a very familiar example. Counting songs are widely used to help children remember the order of number words and virtually every child is able to sing

'A, B, C, D, E, F, G

H, I, J, K, L, M, N, O, P....'.

Learning in this way does not of course guarantee understanding - we have all heard children sing the crucial words or letters in the wrong order - but songs can undoubtedly provide children with a reference point as they become more proficient in getting the words in the right order.

A Canadian researcher, Kieran Egan (1988), takes this idea further. He suggests that for young children (in common with other non-literate groups), music, song, rhyme, story and dance act as 'tools for thinking'. This term is also used by American researcher, Barbara Rogoff (2003). Their theories underline the value of using music, song and dance – all of which are powerful tools for thinking – in learning and teaching phonics. Young children may use these modes of thought to help them do this in the same way as we often use writing or talk to help us sort out complex or puzzling ideas.

Similar ideas are to be found in the work of educators in Reggio Emilia, in Northern Italy - where they speak of 'the hundred languages of children'. The curriculum there rests on the philosophy that translating an idea from one mode of representation to another supports learning and understanding.

A great deal has been written about music and the ways in which it has supported the development of communication, both in the human species and in individuals. With a biological focus, music has been used to enable communication where it would otherwise be difficult. Think of yodelling or drumming – where musical elements have traditionally been used to carry information over great distances. A more immediate example is that adults commonly use a musical chant to summon children from a distance. Children will recognise the tune or intonation of the call, even if they are too far away to distinguish the actual words.

However music doesn't only facilitate communication over distances. It is used by human beings to convey ideas which we would find hard to put into words. Victor Hugo, the French novelist, summed up this aspect of music by suggesting that it allows us to communicate those things which are hard to voice but which we find it impossible to keep silent. He had expressions of love in mind, but many feelings, including protest and revolution, may be conveyed in songs and music.

Music is employed naturally by adults to support communication with babies. Aware that babies do not yet have understanding of spoken language, we use a variety of musical elements to engage the interest and attention of young babies. We raise the pitch of our voices, exaggerate the way in which we vocalise words and vary the speed and loudness of what we say. Often we adopt a repetitive sing-song. These devices or strategies are readily apparent in nursery songs such as *Walking round the garden* but they are by no means unique to English songs. In fact these elements are found in communication with babies around the world (Trevarthen 1998). No one teaches adults to do this. We do it naturally and spontaneously because we see that it evokes response.

Music has also been shown to contribute to learning and development in a number of other fundamental ways. As well as supporting the evolution of communication, music encourages rhythmic movement, a 'vestibular action' (Eliot, 1999) beneficial to young babies because it stimulates the brain. The rhythmic action which is stimulated by music creates pathways in the brain which promote effective learning, while the playful and potentially creative nature of music make learning more likely to occur. The fact is that music acts as a tool for thinking throughout our lives, and we remain aware of it from sometime before our birth until death itself. Hearing is the last sense to be relinquished when we sleep, and the last to leave us when we die.

Learning occurs when connections are made between something familiar and something new. Since the earliest learning or connections are physical or sensory, all abstract thinking must be preceded by learning which makes such connections possible. The sense of fun and enjoyment that music arouses is vital to learning because changes in the chemistry of the brain when we're having fun make learning more likely to occur. Above all, it has been suggested (Mithen, 2005; Lewis Williams, 2002) that music is the source or beginning of all creativity in human development. Experts in human development tell us that in the development of the

 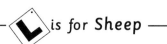

species music almost certainly preceded graphic communication. The voice has been identified as a child's first toy (Papousek, 1994) and play emanates from the vocal experimentation which is characteristic of young babies. Gurgling, babbling and giggles are the precursors of all other play, and like all other play offer opportunities to develop socially and emotionally. In both stimulating and expressing the imagination, sound enables children to develop abstract thinking and creativity.

Why use music to support the learning and teaching of phonics?

The importance of music to learning and development underlines its importance to the learning and teaching of phonics. Like all teaching, if it is to be effective the teaching of phonics must take full account of children's need for

- fun and playfulness
- a balance of adult-directed and child-initiated learning opportunities
- a wide literary experience – including stories, poems and songs
- opportunities for using a range of creative and expressive media.

Effective learning in young children must take account of all aspects of their development. Learning to be literate, including knowledge of phonics, will be enhanced by using music, song and dance because they

- create a relaxed and happy mood
- enable children to feel part of a learning group
- support memory
- offer tools for thinking
- promote communication
- encourage physical movement which stimulates the brain and lays down learning pathways
- enhance imagination and creativity.

The place of the emotions is crucial to all learning. Music enables children to express and experience emotions in ways that might be beyond them linguistically. It helps to prevent the teaching from becoming too staid or uninteresting. Bored children (or adults) do not learn well – music can help to make learning and teaching joyful, reflecting the natural exuberance of young children when engaged and excited by learning. Social interaction, closely linked to emotional well-being, is also vital to effective learning – since humans are essentially social beings. In contributing to group cohesion, music gives children attractive opportunities to participate in the social aspects of literacy. Enjoying something enjoyed by a group of peers is a great motivator and contributes to a positive experience.

As we have shown, music is important to young children since early infancy – and, it has been argued, since before birth. Thus it is a powerful channel for their learning. So how exactly can it help children develop competence in phonics? To begin with, music provides a mechanism for memorising lists and facts – including phonics. It can be of particular value where communication is difficult; for example, in supporting children who are learning English as an additional language, those who are experiencing difficulty in language development, and those who have general learning difficulties. However, we should not fall into the trap of thinking that music, song and dance are only of value to those who are facing problems – they support the learning of everyone! Since the words of songs are so readily remembered they provide excellent material for supporting children in learning to read.

How can I use music to support the learning and teaching of phonics?

All phonic teaching should rest on what children already know about how print functions, and build on existing phonic knowledge. In addition children need to develop their skills of aural discrimination so that they can tune into the sounds of the language, recognise and reproduce them, and relate them to graphemes. Many of the strategies identified in this section are designed to give children a broad and happy experience in learning how print works, to capture their enthusiasm through materials and topics that are of genuine interest to them and to heighten their awareness of sounds. In the same way as effective development in speaking and listening depends on rich experiences which give children something to communicate about, so instruction in phonics can only be truly effective if it goes alongside a genuine interest in books and reading.

- Books and cards (both commercially produced and home-made) of favourite songs and nursery rhymes encourage children to explore print. Encouraging children to choose their favourites at singing time also aids letter and word recognition. The added advantage that comes from using materials of this sort is that children are more likely to read with intonation and feeling – ensuring that a focus on phonics does not lead to mechanical reciting of the words, 'barking at print', but enhances meaning and understanding.

- Work or play with children at creating songs and rhymes where most words begin with the same letter. These may be modifications of known songs. Tate (2005) suggests for example singing to the tune of 'Frere Jacques' the following words:

'Are you acting, Are you acting, Adam Ant, Adam Ant?'

or

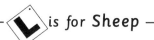 is for **Sheep**

'Are you eating, Are you eating, Eli Eel, Eli Eel?'

The tune of 'Skip to my Lou' can be used to learn the names and sounds of letters of the alphabet:

'A is for apple – ah ah ah

A is for apple – ah ah ah

A is for apple – ah ah ah

This is the letter A.'

'B is for beetle – bh, bh, bh

B is for beetle – bh, bh, bh

B is for beetle – bh, bh, bh

This is the letter B'

Helen McGregor's songbook *Bingo Lingo* is very helpful since it uses known tunes and it's not necessary to be able to read music to make good use of her ideas. She suggests using the tune of 'Polly put the kettle on' to create alliterative verses such as 'Polly puts the pizza in'; 'Sukey sizzles sausages'; 'Anna asks for apple pie' or 'Carli crunched a carrot cake'. Children will come up with any number of other alternatives.

- Children can be encouraged to make up their own songs using repeated alliteration. This has the advantage of promoting and engaging creative energy. Children frequently improvise their own songs (Davies 1994). In addition, many go through a phase of playfully beginning every word in a sentence or chant with the same letter. The resulting nonsense is a source of great fun. These two characteristics can be used to produce phonics materials – writing them out and teaching them to other children.

- Songs focusing on particular letters make use of music's role in supporting memory. The alphabet song mentioned earlier offers a familiar example but there are many others. MacGregor (op.cit.) offers many suggestions, one of which is to focus on vowels sung to the tune of 'The farmer's in the den'. For example:

    The bat and cat are fat,

    The bat and cat are fat,

    A e i o u

    The bat and cat are fat.

    The pet I met got wet....

The pin and bin are tin....

The pot is not so hot.....
The bug will tug the rug...

McGregor also suggests exploring sounds at the beginning and ends of words. For example, to the tune of 'What shall we do with the drunken sailor' she suggests:

What shall we do with the letter d?
What shall we do with the letter d?
What shall we do with the letter d
On this Monday morning?
Let's find words which start with d ...
Desk and door start with d,
Ding and dong start with d,
Do and don't start with d
On this Monday morning.
Let's find words which end with d ...
Send and find end with d,
Hand and stand end with d,
Played and stayed end with d
On this Monday morning.

McGregor also uses the tune of 'Goosey, goosey gander' to explore the sounds of three letter words. One example is:

Make a dog called Dozy,
First you need a d,
O in the middle,
Finish with a g.

Bingo Lingo provides practitioners with a wealth of useful resources. These examples give some ideas to build on and develop.

- Using instruments or body sounds (such as clapping or stamping) to accompany rhyming songs emphasises the similarity of sounds and helps children to maintain a steady beat. Children's awareness of the rhyming sounds is enhanced by the rhythm and this awareness is very important in developing competence as a reader (see Pound and Harrison, 2003). Moreover, there is strong evidence that the development of the ability to copy and maintain a steady beat, 'beat competence', has a powerful positive effect on learning and understanding in general, not simply learning to read.

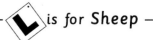 is for **Sheep**

Keeping phonics in their place

It goes without saying that learning to read is of vital importance to an individual's future. The outlook for children who do not acquire adequate reading skills is bleak. They will be barred from access to the wealth of information and ideas, and deprived of the riches of literature. However, it is essential that those of us who know and work with young children keep a sense of proportion. Mastery of phonics is a key element in learning to read, but understanding phonics is not the only thing that children need to learn about reading. Political pressure to focus on phonics must not be allowed to override children's right to grow and develop playfully, to enjoy stories and music. Phonics is a tool not a way of life! Learning to read is hugely important, but it is not the only important thing that children need to do. They need to learn to live and work with others, to develop a sense of self, to enjoy life in the ecstatic manner characteristic of young children and to gain a sense of the world and their place in it.

References

Davies, C. (1994) I can't teach music – so we just sing in Aubrey, C. (ed) *The role of subject knowledge in the early years of schooling.* London, Falmer Press

Egan, K. (1991) Primary understanding. London, Routledge

Eliot, L. (1999) Early intelligence. London, Penguin Books

Lewis-Williams, D. (2002) The mind in the cave. London, Thames and Hudson

McGregor, H. Bingo lingo. London, A&C Black

Mithen, S. (2005) The singing neanderthals. London, Weidenfeld and Nicolson

Papousek, H. (1994) To the evolution of human musicality and musical education, in *Deleige, I. (ed) Proceedings of the 3rd international conference on music perception and cognition.* Liege, ESCOM

Pound, L. and Harrison, C. (2003) Supporting musical development in the early years. Buckingham, Open University Press

Rogoff, B. (2003) The cultural nature of human development. Oxford, Oxford University Press

Tate, M. (2005) Worksheets don't grow dendrites. Thousand Oaks, CA, Corwin Press

Trevarthen, C. (1998) The child's need to learn a culture, in Woodhead, M., Faulkner, D. and Littleton, K. (eds) *Cultural Worlds of Early Childhood.* London, Routledge/ The Open University

L is for Sheep

Margaret Edgington
Why the fuss about phonics?

Margaret Edgington has been an early years teacher, educational home visitor, advisory teacher, and headteacher of a nursery school. She is a member of the Society of Education Consultants and offers a training, advice and consultancy service across the UK, and has worked with nurseries, schools, Children's Centres, local authorities, voluntary groups and universities. She writes on the subject of early childhood education and is author of several books, including *The Foundation Stage Teacher in Action*, 3rd edition, Paul Chapman, 2004; *The Nursery Teacher in Action*, Paul Chapman, 1998 and *The Great Outdoors*, Early Education, 2002. She edited *Interpreting the National Curriculum at Key Stage One: A Developmental Approach*, Open University Press, 1998, and contributed as a writer to *Curriculum Guidance for the Foundation Stage* (QCA/DFEE: 2000). She is a Vice President of Early Education and of the National Campaign for Nursery Education.

In light of the ongoing debate about early literacy and the use of phonics in teaching young children to read, Margaret Edgington argues the importance of allowing young children to be children rather than employing unsuitable teaching methods to force them too soon into inappropriate learning. No quick fix or single approach can work. We must continue listening to individual children and talking with them.

Apart from a few minor amendments to reflect the changing scene, this article first appeared in Early Education, Spring 2006. We thank The British Association for Early Childhood Education for permission to reprint it here.

This article is based on a meeting I led for Early Education's London branch in September 2005. I was asked to provide the arguments for and against phonics teaching to help members who were battling against inappropriate, top-down pressure in their schools. As I did in London, I want to make it clear that I am a specialist in early childhood education, not a literacy specialist. I had to visit a large number of websites to inform myself about the phonics debate.

My experience of phonics teaching began in the late 1960s when, on teaching practice, I was required to use the Initial Teaching Alphabet (ITA). This new phonetic alphabet, which was taught until about the age of 7 at which point it was replaced by traditional English spelling, was thought to be just what we all needed to get children reading quickly. Initially it appeared to work well and there was considerable enthusiasm for extending the ITA across all schools. But then disaster struck as children found it difficult to move from ITA to the less regular spelling of the English language.

Ever since, I have been wary of anything that is presented to us as a quick fix. In my experience quick fixes usually lead to a great deal of repair work later on.

Why the fuss about phonics?

The current focus on phonics teaching was strengthened by some apparently excellent results achieved by children in Clackmannanshire, Scotland, who had been taught through a synthetics phonics approach *Fast Phonics First* (see www.phonicsteaching.com). These results hit the national press in early 2005 and immediately there were calls for all children to be taught using synthetic phonics. In June 2005 Ruth Kelly, Secretary of State for Education, appointed former HMI Jim Rose to lead a review of 'best practice in the teaching of early reading and the range of strategies that best support children who have fallen behind in reading to catch up'. In this review Mr Rose was asked to consider

1. what our expectations of best practice in the teaching of early reading and synthetic phonics should be for primary schools and early years settings, including both the content and the pace of teaching

2. how this relates to the development of the birth to five framework and the ongoing development and renewal of the National Literacy Framework for teaching

3. what range of provision best supports children with significant literacy difficulties and enables them to catch up with their peers, and the relationship of such targeted intervention programmes with synthetic phonics teaching.

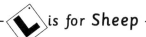

The time-scale allowed for the review was extremely short. The Rose Report appeared in an interim version late in 2005 and in its final form in March 2006. The report reached a number of recommendations and conclusions, which may be summarised as follows:

- phonic work is often a 'neglected or weak feature' of the teaching of reading
- best practice for early readers provides them with 'a rich curriculum that fosters all four interdependent strands of language: speaking, listening, reading and writing'
- systematic phonic work 'that is matched to their developing abilities enables (children) to benefit from the wealth of opportunities afforded by reading from an early age'
- '*despite uncertainties in research findings*' (our italics, Ed.) synthetic phonics 'offers the vast majority of young children the best and most direct route to becoming skilled readers and writers'
- well designed programmes for teaching and learning phonics systematically 'converge around a small number of core principles'
- it is important for parents, carers, setting and schools to stimulate children's early interest in literacy 'by exploiting play, stories, songs and rhymes and provide lots of opportunities, and time, to talk with children about their experiences and feelings'
- training for practitioners at all levels is important
- settings and schools have 'at least sufficient and often good material resources for teaching reading, including phonic work'.

It is worth stressing that the report recommended that phonic work 'should be set within a broad and rich language curriculum', and that 'for most children, high quality, systematic phonic work should start by the age of five'; i.e. not at three or barely four.

However, the reference to synthetic phonics in the context of early years settings and the birth to five framework rang alarm bells, and many nursery teachers have expressed concern that they are now being asked to start formal phonics teaching programmes with three year olds, some of whom may have had little experience of sharing books prior to entering the nursery.

In the rest of this chapter I want to provide some facts about phonics teaching and some evidence on what helps children to learn to read effectively and become avid lifelong readers. I will then highlight some priorities we need to focus on in the foundation stage.

Some facts about phonics

The debate around phonics teaching focuses on the difference between using an 'analytic phonics' approach or the 'synthetic phonics' approach (see www.literacytrust.org.uk). The main features of these two approaches are:

Analytic phonics

1. *Involves analysis of whole words to detect phonetic or spelling patterns.*
2. *Teaches the sounds of letters in the context of words – children learn to break words down rather than build them up.*
3. *Considers 'onset' (initial phoneme) and 'rime' (rest of word).*
4. *Works particularly well with words which cannot easily be worked out sound by sound.*
5. *Uses the rime of words to help children read and spell by analogy, eg. would, could, should.*
6. *Taught in a mixture with a whole-language approach.*
7. *An efficient way to help children develop a large sight vocabulary for reading and spelling.*

Synthetic phonics

1. *Starts with phonemic awareness and mapping sound to letter/s.*
2. *Shows how sounds of letters can be blended (or synthesised) to produce different words.*
3. *Children learn phonemes (the smallest unit of sound) and their grapheme (their written symbol or symbols eg 'ow' and 'ough'). On the internet, I found different websites mentioned a different number of phonemes to be learnt!*
4. *Children learn to build up words rather than break them down.*
5. *A particularly useful approach with phonetically regular words.*
6. *Involves a highly systematic whole class-teaching programme plus group work.*
7. *Involves a multi-sensory approach, with children seeing the symbol, listening to the sound, saying the sound and accompanying this by doing an action.*

Critics of analytic phonics say the approach takes too long to help children decode text, relies too heavily on guesswork and is confusing for children. It is, however, an approach recognised by early years practitioners. Many young children get into phonics by noticing that meaningful words (such as their names) start with the same letter sounds or end in the same letter strings.

Critics of synthetic phonics say it is boring and meaningless, does not suit all learning styles, and enables children to decode, but not necessarily to understand

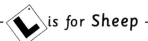
is for Sheep

and enjoy, what they are reading. In a recent edition of Dispatches, a 10-year-old child with Down's Syndrome was shown decoding complex words but clearly not understanding what she was reading (Mills: 2005).

What helps young children learn to read – messages from research

The following points, drawn from recent research, should help practitioners provide an evidence-based rationale for resisting inappropriate pressure.

1. Young children (younger than five or six) do not thrive on a formal, whole-class approach to teaching – they need an approach which embeds literacy learning in meaningful contexts (POST: 2000).

2. Children exposed to formal teaching may make progress in the short term but this is not always lasting. Children taught the same things up to three years later make just as good if not better progress in the long term (Sharp: 2003).

3. Home-educated children often start to read very late, perhaps not until they are eight or nine, but they become avid, enthusiastic readers (Thomas: 1998).

4. Studies on the positive effects of synthetic-phonics teaching show that this work was started with children who were at least four years and six months old. In Scotland, children start school in the September after they have turned four and a half. Assuming a settling-in period, the children would probably be four years and eight months before the synthetics phonics programme starts. The Fast Phonics First programme requires that children enter primary school knowing how to hold a book and turn the pages, where to start and in which direction to go, and about the vocabulary of reading.

5. Formal teaching strategies may damage children's later enjoyment of reading. NFER research found that, although English children read well, there has been a significant reduction in enjoyment of reading since the introduction of the National Literacy Strategy (Berliner: 2005).

In the light of this evidence it is clear that starting synthetic-phonics teaching with children younger than about five is counter-productive. Because young boys tend to be kinaesthetic learners – they need to move to learn – a formal whole-class approach may particularly disadvantage them.

So what should we prioritise in the foundation stage?

The following points are raised to remind practitioners of some important priorities when supporting children's literacy development. Practitioners need to:

1. recognise that one approach will not work for every child – it is vital to

observe and listen to individuals, to tune into their developmental needs, interests and learning styles, using the *Curriculum Guidance for the Foundation Stage* (QCA: 2000) to support differentiation

2. work in partnership with parents to help them understand more about the development of communication, language and literacy

3. make time for sustained listening to and conversing with children – in order to read and write children need to be able to listen and use rich language

4. tell, read and re-enact a wide range of stories and books, including books from a wide range of cultural traditions – storytelling is particularly useful to fire children's imaginations

5. encourage children to develop a wide repertoire of songs and rhymes and to keep a steady beat – encouraging play with rhyme and words

6. provide positive role models to demonstrate reading and writing skills (adults or older children) – young children need to see the point of reading and writing

7. scribe children's talk and stories so they can become authors of their own books

8. play games such as 'I Spy' or 'Simon Says' to focus on rhyme or sounds ('I spy with my little eye something which rhymes with ...' and 'Simon says find something which starts with ...')

9. encourage children's awareness of phonemes, eg my name starts with ...

These practices will provide children with a firm foundation for later literacy teaching. Children who have not had this experience will inevitably flounder later.

In their useful book *Foundations of Literacy*, Sue Palmer and Ros Bayley (2004) highlight a 'seven-stranded approach' to literacy development, with a strong emphasis on communication, speaking and listening as the foundation for reading and writing. They emphasise that in order to develop phonological awareness ('tuning into sound') children first need to have learnt to listen. This involves:

1. discrimination of sound – a foreground sound against background noise

2. social listening – looking at the person talking, remembering and responding to what is said, turn-taking in conversation

3. developing aural attention span

4. developing auditory memory – remembering songs and rhymes, keeping a steady beat.

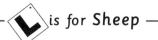 **L** is for **Sheep**

Once children have developed these four skills they are able to tune into sound which, according to Palmer and Bayley, involves:

1. phonological awareness – the awareness of words as units of sound, of syllables (ie words can be made up of several sounds), and of rhyme
2. phonemic awareness – the awareness of individual speech sounds
3. phonics – sound–symbol associations.

In light of the recent discussion regarding national results for the Foundation Stage Profile (Ward: 2005) – which unsurprisingly indicate that, for the third year running, a minority of children achieved the early learning goals for literacy (28% for writing. 36% in reading) – it is surely time to argue for practitioners in the foundation stage to focus on the priorities outlined above and to be released from the pressure of chasing unrealistic literacy goals. I hope all practitioners will contribute their views to the reviews of the National Literacy Strategy and to the Early Development and Learning Framework. We need to recognise that we now have a crucial opportunity to get it right for the young children we all care about.

References

Berliner, W. (2005) War of Words, *Education Guardian, 5 April.*

Mills, D. (producer) (2005) The Dyslexia Myth, in *Dispatches*, Channel4, broadcast 8 September.

Palmer, S. & Bayley, R. (2004) Foundations of Literacy: a balanced approach to language, listening and literacy skills in the early years. Stafford, Network Educational Press Ltd.

POST (2000) Early Years Learning. POST report 140 (June), Parliamentary Office of Science and Technology *(see www.parliament.uk/post/pn140.pdf).*

QCA (2000) Curriculum guidance for the foundation stage. London, QCA/DfEE.

Sharp, C. (2003) School Starting Age: European policy and recent research, *Early Education, issue 39, pp. 7-10.*

Thomas, A. (1998) Educating Children at Home. London, Cassell.

Ward, H. (2005) Early Goals Out of Reach. *Times Educational Supplement*, 21 October.

L is for Sheep

Janet Moyles
Is everybody ready?

Janet Moyles is Emeritus Professor of Education at Anglia Ruskin University and an early years consultant. Working intially with young children through the playgroup movement, she trained as an early years teacher, and worked in nursery, first and primary school education for many years before becoming first a headteacher, then a senior lecturer in early childhood education at the University of Leicester. She followed this with a period as professor of early childhood education, involving herself extensively in teaching and research.

Janet has published widely on issues related to early years practice, especially play and practitioner roles. She has written for numerous magazines and among other works is author of *The Excellence of Play* (Open University Press, 2005), *Images of Violence* (with Sîan Adams, Featherstone Education, 2005), and *Organising for Learning in the Primary Classroom* (Open University Press, 1992).

In this section Janet describes her concerns that in their pre-occupation with standards of achievement, policy makers may be forcing practitioners into adopting approaches which are too formal too soon, which includes over emphasis on learning phonics. She argues that children learn best in a supportive environment which recognises their individual needs, and that there are stages of readiness for various aspects of learning; attempts to drum learning into a child before the relevant stage has been reached are doomed to frustration and failure. It is the task of the trained practitioner to recognise these stages and manage the appropriate learning.

It is a continuing frustration that, despite all the research evidence to the contrary, many of those responsible for policy making in early childhood education and care still place heavy emphasis on 'formal' teaching methods in literacy for young children. This is open to wide misunderstanding and misinterpretation by the broad range of people who staff early years settings, not least because many have not been trained specifically in the teaching of language and reading skills, in child development, or in teaching and learning through play. All of these, in my view, are vital prerequisites to understanding how children learn to read and to write.

Many early years teachers and other practitioners know from their training and their significant experience of observing young children's activities that for young children learning phonics should be about playing with the components of language and enjoying its complexity. They understand the importance of teaching in such a way as to engage children in the excitement of speaking, listening, mark-making and immersing themselves in the richness of language. This applies equally to first and additional languages and to the celebration of bi-lingual and multi-lingual talents. It is the joy of language which needs to be inculcated and not isolated into 'formal' individual skills. Literacy learning is not about providing endless worthless worksheets which, at best, show what children already know and at worst encourage children to think that learning to read and write are chores best avoided (Dombey: 2006). If we do not excite and stimulate children they may never know the delights of independent reading. Some groups of children are at particular risk from an inappropriate emphasis on formal teaching, including many boys, those in the early stages of learning English, and children with special social or educational needs.

Policies or schemes which adopt a 'one size fits all' approach – a single method of teaching phonics which can be applied to all children irrespective of their different ways of learning or their cultural backgrounds – are simply inappropriate, as I hope to show in this chapter. This method is antithetical to all the positive moves that have been made in recent years to develop more appropriate, child-oriented curricular practices. Children under the age of five or six thrive on approaches that embed learning in meaningful contexts (Blakemore: 2000). Indeed, Paragraph 2 of the *The Early Years Foundation Stage: Direction of Travel* document (2005) states clearly:

> *The approach of practitioners will be age appropriate, ensuring that there are different activities for children of different ages and at different stages of their development. Through the EYFS parents can feel secure knowing that all settings will allow children to progress at a pace that's right for them as individuals.*

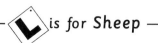 is for **Sheep**

Surely, practices in literacy must follow these principles of appropriateness and flexibility? There are numerous researchers who emphasise this need, not least Harrison (2004) and David et al. (2000). Young children are entitled to education and care that is relevant to them now. What is important is that children have a childhood unencumbered by pressures to conform to later expectations. The child's early experiences of language and literacy are not merely a preparation for what is to come but an exciting time in which skills, knowledge and understandings are being developed and interest and enthusiasm generated. If we get this wrong we risk an alienation that will be hard to remedy later. Young children do not need to be put under pressure to learn; if the learning is appropriate to their existing skills, knowledge and understanding they will take to it with enthusiasm.

A powerful message is given in BERA's extensive review of early years literature in 2003. In interrogating literacy research, the writers conclude:

> This review ... has affirmed young children as active literacy learners and problem solvers who are able to engage in the formidable task of making sense of a complex system of spoken and written language. The evidence available supports the view that in the earlier years this is most likely to take place in a literacy rich environment where learning is support by a receptive and psychologically available adult (p.28).

In this article, I set out the arguments for ensuring that all approaches to literacy learning, and in particular to phonics, must start from a basis of what we already know about how children learn and which methods best suit individuals. I will go on to examine related issues such as the roles of practitioners in supporting language and literacy development. Throughout, I will explore current research which helps to explain why a particular approach to phonics and literacy learning is recommended. Factors such as the influences of child development on literacy learning and early cognition, international experiences and research, the affective power of story and literature and the socio-cultural dimensions of literacy will implicitly be explored.

Understanding children's development and literacy learning

I must state at the outset that I am *not* against phonics teaching per se: there is a place for alphabetic and phonological awareness to be learned and taught. Learning to write and to spell helps reading, and the three strands support each other as children move through Key Stage 1. My concern is *how* this is likely to take place, and the climate and manner in which children will best learn to be literate. Phonics is an important strand of learning to read and write, but I would argue that it is taught more effectively when children are older, and able to learn the rules quickly and without confusion. There is little logic in expecting a child who is not yet able to pronounce words clearly to be able to decode or encode phonetically. Therefore, in all early learning but especially in teaching phonics, understanding the developmental capacities of the child is the vital first step. As an example, hearing the differences between the sounds of the consonants **b**, **d** and **t** (auditory discrimination) is hard for many adults, let alone children, especially in the context of group work in a (sound-filled) setting or classroom. Distinguishing between the written forms of **b** and **d** and **p**, which are different only in orientation, is yet another skill, this time of visual acuity.

The learner has to be the main focus of teaching in early childhood, where developing confidence and a disposition to learning – as well as learning how to learn – are inescapable. And we know that there is no *one* way to teach any individual child to read and write – no set formula – an inarguable conclusion highlighted by so many researchers and writers (e.g. Wells: 1985; Wyse and Jones: 2001; Whitehead: 2002; Gillen and Hall: 2004; Palmer and Bayley: 2004; Broadhead: 2003). We must hold firm to this wisdom, whatever civil servants try to tell us. Learning to read and write is a very complex process, made all the more difficult by individual children approaching the task very differently, depending upon their learning style, their disposition to learning and their prior literacy experiences (McBride-Chang: 2004). Confidence and competence in speaking, listening and social interactions are the most important underpinning skills (Brooker: 2002; Broadhead: 2003; Palmer and Bayley: 2004).

Developmentally, a significant number of children in the 3-6 age-range are simply not ready for formal instruction in reading skills. As one example, my elder son read and could apply phonics at the age of three and a half: my other son (who gained a 2:1 degree and now owns his own company) did not learn to read until he was eight, and struggled to acquire phonic knowledge, despite systematic teaching in the primary school and additional support from an excellent private tutor. This latter son was tested by a school psychologist who could find no specific intellectual problem – his eventual diagnosis was that this child failed to read because he simply was not ready to understand sentences, words or letters. Neither did he have a 'disposition' to learn to read as a young child. And this from a home which was awash with books!

For long it has been known that children (and adults) do not learn incrementally but rather more idiosyncratically and 'messily'. Support for this comes from any number of writers on psychology and, more recently, from those who investigate the relationship between brain studies and children's learning; for example see Hannaford: 1995; Kotulak: 1996; Sylwester: 1997; Claxton: 1997; Costello: 2000; Gardner: 1999; Coles: 2003. Learning is an 'untidy' business and, as

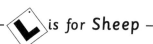
is for **Sheep**

every practitioner knows, with young children happens in the most unexpected ways and at varied times. Notoriously, too, young children will know something one day and in one context and have mislaid that knowledge on another day, when something of greater importance to the child will have been overlaid on to the earlier activity. Good literature, favourite books, poems, songs, music, drama, physical activity and other multi-sensory approaches, all have a major part to play in young children becoming fluent readers with positive attitudes towards learning literacy and learning in general. Playing with words has long been known to be of enormous importance in children developing a rich vocabulary (see e.g. Moyles: 1989; Marsh and Hallett: 1999; Whitehead: 2002). An interest in books and pictures is also a vital pre-requisite – many children are still exploring these elements when they start Key Stage 1, let alone in the current Foundation Stage, and certainly books and rhymes are key factors in engaging the under threes in language. Any teaching which takes away the emphasis from the story and the child making meaning from the pictures and language is unlikely to produce effective readers and writers who enjoy, are inspired by and learn from books.

What the child can do has to be the starting point for all early years teaching and learning (see e.g. Bruce: 2005; Gardner: 1999). Writing, too, should start from children's current interests and abilities. What many children can do, for example, is make marks, and draw and play with a range of sounds and drawn shapes, the starting point for writing (e.g. Riley and Reedy: 2000; Hall and Robinson: 1998; Mathews: 2003). It is through these activities that the child will gain enough confidence and sufficient physical co-ordination and manipulation skills to, eventually and gradually, produce more formal writing.

Knowing the letters of the alphabet can easily be achieved by very young children. Many bright early learners can recite the names of the letters, just as they can say numbers up to ten or twenty. But this does not usually mean that they understand their meaning and significance. Knowing the word 'eight' and being able to place it in a sequence does not necessarily mean that the child understands the concept of 'eightness'. Similarly, understanding the relationship of letters to, and within, words is a very different skill from simply memorising the alphabet, or even being able to give the name of a letter when shown its shape. At two and a half years, my grandson could happily 'parrot' the alphabet as part of a game we played, but became totally confused if he was asked to identify individual letters: the activity made no sense to him at all – the flow and sound of the alphabet was what interested him. Many children older than this suffer equal confusion when presented with sounds, letter patterns, phonemes and such like unless they are directly related to something which 'makes human sense' (in Margaret Donaldson's words) to the young learner. Yet equally there are many excellent young readers who gain nothing by enforced phonic instruction: as Wyse (2005) suggests in his web-based paper (http://www.tactyc.org.uk/pdfs/wyse.pdf)

> *... many children are ready for a focus on print and text and we do them a disservice if we resist this ... [but] children who can already read do not need a phonics programme; their reading should be developed in other ways. This necessitates a differentiated approach in early years classrooms where all children will benefit from an emphasis on the sharing of high quality texts but some will be ready for a more direct focus on print and text ...*

While developing these skills as competent and confident readers and writers, children need a combination of varied and exciting play-based activities to promote a wide range of literacy skills. As Hall (2005: 87) sugggests:

> *Within realistic play settings, literacy is not fragmented by artificial instructional processes. Literacy is used for whatever is appropriate in the play: going shopping, having a meal in a restaurant, going on a train journey, visiting a hospital and so on. The literacy occurs because it is needed in the context of the play, not because instruction demands it.*

A diet of drills and skills has never worked to motivate most young children (see Anning 1997); they simply turn off, which is potentially disadvantaging even more children. As Dombey (2006) assserts:

> *Young children have great difficulty in recognising that words are composed of sequences of separable phonemes. ... Games of 'I-spy' with four-year-olds can be frustrating. It's even harder for them to identify the final and medial phonemes of a word than it is to say what the word begins with. (p.6)*

Boys notoriously learn better when physically and actively engaged in the process (see, e.g. Connolly: 2004). Many reading and writing activities undertaken in classrooms and settings as a result of the National Literacy Strategy rely on much seat-based work which requires the child to listen and, occasionally, to respond (see examples in Adams et al.: 2004). For example, in my experience many 'big book' sessions are turgid examples of adults demolishing text and text-related structures, rather than gaining children's interest in the story and understanding how different children might receive it.

For most young children who 'fail' at phonics, it will be because they don't yet have the language skills, visual/auditory acuity or tongue development necessary to sound out or understand the structure of words. Children for whom English is not a first language will have different needs, e.g. their (and their families) pronunciation of letters and words will often differ significantly from those presented by the practitioner.

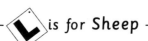
is for **Sheep**

It is worth acknowledging, too, that any failure to read by children in the UK could be because they are unique internationally in beginning school before they are five years old. In other countries they are not expected to start formal learning until they are six or more, even in languages where links between sounds and letters are more predictable than English, a point to which I shall now turn.

The English language and and its phonological challenges

Our writing system is alphabetic. The alphabet, when translated into sounds, is inconsistent and downright idiosyncratic. If they were to rely heavily on the alphabetic sounds it is highly unlikely that young children would make much sense of many of the words they need to read and write. One only has to consider words like 'school' and 'church' or 'know' and 'now'. Even spelling simple words 'synthetically' is fraught with problems: it is impossible to articulate consonants without adding 'uh', e.g. b = buh, t = tuh. Buh - a - tuh does not sound out 'bat' (it sounds more like 'butter'!). It takes very specific teaching and articulation strategies to show children how to sound-out individual letters in order to blend or sythesise them (encoding) or to break them down (decoding). Consider how difficult basic words such as 'could' and 'because' become with a synthetic phonics approach. Analytic phonics allows for far greater opportunity for understanding, e.g. 'at' (as a word and as a rime) can be added to 'h', 'b', 'c' and other letters readily, and can contribute to rhyming sounds amongst other things. It also offers an efficient way for children to develop a large sight vocabulary for reading and spelling alongside mixed sensory and kinaesthetic approaches. In addition,

> ...English-speaking children develop a variety of recoding strategies, supplementing grapheme-phoneme conversion strategies with the recognition of letter patterns for rimes ... and attempts at whole-word recognition (unique spelling patterns such as "choir" and "people") must be learned as whole words. (Goswami 2005: 277/8)

The complexities which abound in using English as a phonetic language are legion. As adults we find many spellings complex, confusing and frustrating – when you first heard the word 'tsunami' what letter did you think it began with? How much worse (and inadequate) must a young child feel who struggles with words such as 'war' and 'car', 'who' and 'shoe' or 'sew' and 'so'. As Henrietta Dombey (2006: 6) points out:

> Perhaps the greatest problem is that many English spellings simply do not fit with the idea of one to one correspondence between letter and phoneme. It's not really possible to 'sound out' such common words as 'one', 'was' and 'all'. The vowels are the real problem. English is vowel-rich, having 20 vowels or diphthongs (as against, for example, the 12 of Spanish). But we have only the

same 5 letters (or 6 if you include 'y') to represent them. The letter 'a' stands for quite different vowel sounds in the words 'cat', 'car', 'came', 'call' and 'career'.

Going further, Goswami (2005), in her scholarly paper, shows clearly that:

... relying solely on grapheme-phoneme correspondences leads to inefficient recording of English. There are so many irregular words that it may be difficult or impossible to access meaning by recoding letters into phonemes. (p.277)

This is particularly so with the English language, as opposed to other international languages, including Welsh, which have a far greater sound/symbol correspondence (see Ellis and Hooper 2001). Quoting a number of internationally renowned research studies, Goswami (2005) states:

The evidence from these studies is that learning to read English is a more difficult learning task than learning to read Finnish, Spanish or Italian. This makes it inherently unlikely that one method of teaching phonics will suddenly cause English children to perform like Finnish children' [who, in any case, do not begin formal schooling until they are seven years of age]. '... The reduced consistency of the English writing system in both reading and spelling is a key factor in explaining the dramatic differences in reading acquisition across languages ... English is particularly inconsistent with respect to the small reading units emphasised by synthetic phonics ... (p.276)

So both children's development and the English language itself, create significant challenges for practitioners working within the Foundation Stage.

Practitioners and literacy teaching

Playful 'pick and mix' has been the way of teaching young children successfully for many years: they thrive on variety for the simple reason that each child learns in his own way, dependent upon the factors above and also including their own socio-cultural, literacy and communication experiences and their existing intellectual understanding. Formal teaching strategies can often spoil children's enjoyment of the reading process and dampen a child's natural excitement in the early stages of being able to decode print. An NFER report suggests a significant reduction in enjoyment of reading since the introduction of the National Literacy Strategy (Berliner: 2005).

Comments I've received from teachers and other practitioners recently and over many years, support the view that the teaching of reading and writing involves mixed approaches, focusing on interesting, stimulating and appropriate child-oriented activities.

is for Sheep

The government's flagship early years research, the EPPE (Effective Provision of Pre-School Education) project, has reported a major finding in the need for 'sustained shared thinking' between young children and practitioners (Sylva et al.: 2004). This research provides a powerful argument that the most effective learning is heavily dependent on the practitioner working *with* the child to extend his/her present thinking and knowledge across the curriculum. Enforcing a specific method of literacy teaching upon reflective practitioners robs them of their professionalism and risks demoralising them by requiring them to undertake activities which they feel are inappropriate to their children's learning needs. Practitioners must be empowered to make their own decisions about individual children in line with the new EYFS directives.

Training in literacy learning and teaching is a vital issue, particularly given the diversity of practitioners' background. The best practitioners also need support from – and to give support to – parents. Many researchers have shown the immense benefits of parental involvement and partnership in children's developing literacy skills and in their enjoyment of books and reading; one reason why many schools send books home with children for sharing with parents and carers (e.g. Nutbrown et al.: 2005). There are, however, difficulties in ensuring that parents successfully support children's learning of phonics alongside practitioners. In fact, one could argue that being taught differently by a variety of adults could prove to be disastrous for children just getting to grips with the nuances of letter/sound relationships. Care should be taken to ensure that parents have sensitive guidance and support in making their contribution to the child's learning.

Research impacting upon early literacy learning

Results nationally from the *Foundation Stage Profile* (Ward: 2005) show that, for the third year running, only a minority of children have achieved the early learning goals for literacy (26% for writing and 36% for reading). A consistently low proportion of children succeed in reaching the early learning goal on linking sounds to letters and also the goals for reading and writing. There are several probable reasons for this.

1. These goals (along with one for mathematical calculation) are arguably unrealistically high, having been set originally at the equivalent of Level 1 in the National Curriculum to meet the demands of the National Literacy Strategy.

2. Too much of the NLS teaching implemented in Reception and Year 1 classes shows young children spending significant amounts of time without the sorts of interactions with adults or with each other for which I have argued above, and which early years professionals know work. Far

too much time is spent on 'passive' listening. In one study (Adams et al.: 2004) it was found that individual four year old children sat for a minimum of 54 minutes during a day 'listening' to the teacher without the opportunity for any response other than hand-raising.

The conclusions of the Education Select Committee's (2004) report on teaching children to read acknowledged the importance of teaching phonics, but not for children before five. It recommended that the DfES should commission further research into early reading. The Select Committee, however, heard evidence, in the main, only from those who support a synthetic phonics approach: there was a significant dearth of those who disagreed with that approach and who have substantive evidence that other approaches are more effective and more appropriate to young learners. In the American Reading Panel Report it was found that synthetic phonics was no better than other phonics approaches. In a recent article Dr. Morag Stuart (who gave evidence to the Select Committee) comments that ...

> ...after more than thirty years of research effort, no adequate test has yet been made of the hypothesis that phoneme awareness actually does influence the development of reading (2005: 48).

In a very recent government funded piece of research into literacy learning, Torgeson et al. (2006) found only one study that involved children under five years of age and there was no evidence to support the systematic teaching of phonics to children under five. As the authors state:

> The main findings of this review do not support the view that any children who have not yet started to read at school entry should immediately receive systematic phonics teaching.

Conclusion

Many young children learn about phonics firstly by relating meaning to the letters in their own names. Later they go on to notice other words with similar letter sounds or letter strings. They learn to do this in association with and supported by sensitive and committed adults, both practitioners and parents. There is a stage at which children's developing brains are ready for these skills, and no amount of rushing children into reading will produce a nation of readers: in fact it may well have the reverse effect. Many researchers, such as Goleman (1996), Bruner (1996), Postman (1994), Elkind (1988) and others have shown clearly the dangers of attempting to teach young children processes for which they are developmentally, culturally, socially or cognitively unprepared. Older children often get the idea of phonics quickly and easily, once they are confident in their abilities to handle books and reading. Young children do not, and for that there are reasons

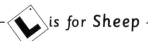 is for Sheep

that are nothing to do with methods or fads.

Phonics, as we have seen, may enable some children to decode: but will they understand and enjoy what they read? The latter should surely be a major aim of any literacy programme. The emotional/affective aspects of story telling and story sharing are easily forgotten when the focus is on 'accelerating' children's acquisition of reading sub-skills and, as we all know, the disposition to read (and the enjoyment of reading) can easily be compromised by this urge to hurry children along. Let us not be party to doing this to young children in England: they deserve better.

References

Adams, S., et al. (2004) Inside the Foundation Stage. Re-creating the reception year. London, Association of Teachers and Lecturers.

Anning, A. (1997) The First Years at School. Buckingham, Open University Press.

Barratt-Pugh, C. and Rohl, M. (eds) (2001) Literacy Learning in the Early Years. Buckingham, Open University Press.

Berliner, D. (2005) War of Words. *Education Guardian, 5th April.*

Blakemore, S. (2000) Early Years' Learning, Parliamentary Office for Science and Technology (POST) Report. London, House of Commons POST Report 140 *(see www.parliament.uk/post/home.htm 2000)*

British Education Research Association (BERA) Early Years Special Interest Group (2003) Review of Early Years Research: Pedagogy, Curriculum and Adult Roles. Southwell, Notts, BERA.

Broadhead, P. (2003) Early Years Play and Learning: developing social skills and co-operation. London, Routledge-Falmer.

Brooker, L. (2002) Starting School: young children learning cultures. Buckingham, Open University Press.

Bruce, T. (2005) Early Childhood Education 3rd edn. London, Hodder and Stoughton.

Bruner, J. (1996) The Culture of Education. Camb, Mass, Harvard University Press.

Clark, M. (1976) Young Fluent Readers. London, Heinemann Educational.

Claxton, G. (1997) Hare Brain - Tortoise Mind: why intelligence increases when you think less. London, Fourth Estate.

Claxton, G. and Carr, M. (2004) A framework for teaching and learning: the dynamics of disposition. *Early Years. 24(1), 87-97.*

Coles, G. (2003) Brain Activity, Genetics and Learning to Read. In N. Hall, J. Larson and J. Marsh (eds) *Handbook of Early Childhood Literacy.* London, Sage.

Connolly, P (2004) Boys and Schooling in the Early Years. London, Routledge Falmer.

Costello, P. (2000) Thinking Skills and Early Childhood Education. London, David Fulton

David, T. et al. (2000) <u>Making Sense of Early Literacy</u>. Stoke-on-Trent, Trentham Books.

Department for Education and Skills (2005) <u>Early Years Foundation Stage: Direction of Travel Document</u>. London, DfES.

Dombey, H. (2006) <u>How Should we Teach Children to Read?</u> *Books for Keeps. 156, 6-7.*

Education Select Committee Report (2004) Teaching Children to Read, available at *www.publications.parliament.uk/pa/cm200405/cmselect/cmeduski/121/121.pdf*

Elkind, D. (1988) <u>The Hurried Child</u>. Reading, MA, Addison Wesley.

Ellis, N. and Hooper, A. (2001) <u>Why learning to read is easier in Welsh than in English: orthographic transparency effects evinced with frequency-matched tests</u>. *Applied Psycholinguistics. 22, 571-599.*

Gardner, H. (1999) <u>Intelligence Reframed</u>. New York, Basic Books.

Gillen, J. and Hall, N. (2004) <u>The Emergence of Early Childhood Literacy</u>. In N. Hall, J. Marsh and J. Larson (eds) *Handbook of Early Childhood Literacy.* London, Sage Publications.

Goswami, U. (2005) <u>Synthetic phonics and learning to read: a cross-language perspective</u>. *Educational Psychology in Practice. 21(4), 27-282.*

Hall, J., Marsh, J. and Larson, J. (2000) (eds.) <u>Handbook of Early Childhood Literacy</u>. London, Sage.

Hall, N. (2005) <u>Play, Literacy and Situated Learning</u>. In J. Moyles *The Excellence of Play,* Maidenhead, Open University Press.

Hall, N. and Robinson, A. (1998) <u>Exploring Writing and Play in the Early Years</u>. London, Hodder and Stoughton.

Hannaford, C. (1995) <u>Smart Moves: why learning is not all in your head</u>. Great Ocean Publishers.

Harrison, C. (2004) <u>Understanding Reading Development</u>. London, Paul Chapman.

Holt, J. (1990) <u>Learning All the Time</u>. Ticknell, Education Now.

Kotulak, R. (1996) <u>Inside the Brain: revolutionary discoveries of how the mind works</u>. Kansas City, MO, Andrews and McMeely.

Marsh, J. and Hallett, E. (ed) (1999) <u>Desirable Literacies: approaches to language and literacy in the early years</u>. London, Paul Chapman.

Matthews, J. (2003) <u>Drawing and Painting: children and visual representation</u>. London, Paul Chapman.

McBride-Chang, C. (2004) <u>Children's Literacy Development</u>. London, Hodder Arnold,

Moyles, J. (1989) <u>Just Playing? The Role and Status of Play in Early Childhood Education</u>. Buckingham, Open University Press.

Moyles, J. and Adams, S. (2001) <u>StEPs: Statements of Entitlement to Play</u>. Buckingham, Open University Press.

Nutbrown. C., Hannon, P. and Morgan, A. (2005) <u>Early Literacy Work and Families: policy, practice and research</u>. London, Sage.

Palmer, S. and Bayley, R. (2004) <u>Foundations of Literacy</u>. Stafford, Network Educational Press.

Postman, N. (1994) <u>The Disappearance of Childhood</u>. London, W.H. Allen

Riley, J. and Reedy, D. (eds) (2000) <u>Developing Writing for Different Purposes: teaching about genre in the early years</u>. London, Paul Chapman.

Stuart, M. (2005) <u>Phonemic analysis and reading development: some current issues</u>. *Journal of Research in Reading, 28 (1): 39-49.*

Sylva, K., Melhuish, E., Sammons, P., Siraj-Blatchford, I. and Taggart, B. (2004) <u>The Effective Provision of Pre-School Education (EPPE) Project. Technical Paper 12. The Final Report. Effective Pre-School Education</u>. London, DfES/Institute of Education, University of London.

Sylwester, R. (1997) <u>A Celebration of Neurons: an educator's guide to the human brain</u>. Alexandria, VA, Association for Supervision and Curriculum Development.

Torgeson, C., Brooks, G. and Hall, J. (2006) <u>A Systematic Review of the Research Literature on the Use of Phonics in the Teaching of Reading and Spelling</u>. DfES Research Report No: 711.

Ward, H. (2005) <u>Early Goals Out of Reach</u>. *Times Educational Supplement, 21st October.*

Wells, G. (1985) <u>Language Learning and Education</u>. Windsor, NFER/Nelson.

Whitehead, M. (2002) <u>Developing Language and Literacy with Young Children</u>. 2nd ed. London, Paul Chapman-Sage.

Wood, E. and Attfield, J. (1996) <u>Play, Learning and the Early Childhood Curriculum</u>. London, Paul Chapman.

Wyse, D. and Jones, R. (2001) <u>Teaching English, Language and Literacy</u>. London, Routledge-Falmer.

Results from the Foundation Stage Profile 2005 can be seen on www.dfes.gov.uk/rsgateway/DB/SFR/s000608/index.shtml. The 2004 results are available on www.dfes.gov.uk/rsgateway/DB/SFR/s000566/index.shtml

L is for Sheep

Janet Evans
Reading for writing

Janet Evans is Senior Lecturer in Education at Liverpool Hope University, and a part-time freelance consultant in literacy and education. She teaches post-graduate teacher education courses and provides professional development consultancy to individual teachers and whole schools.

Janet's research interests include critical reader response in the picture story texts genre, process and interactive writing through role-play in the early years, and the impact of popular culture and critical literacies in the primary classroom. She regularly publishes in academic journals and has written and edited widely, including *What's in the Picture: Responding to Illustrations in Picture Books* (Paul Chapman, 1998) and *The Writing Classroom: Aspects of Writing and the Primary Child 3-11years* (David Fulton and Heinemann, 2001) . Her latest book, *Literacy Moves On: Using Popular Culture, New Technologies and Critical Literacy in the Primary Classroom* (2005) is published by David Fulton in England and Heinemann in the USA, and focuses on the changing nature of literacy in the 21st century. Janet is on the review panel for *The Journal of Early Childhood Literacy*, Sage Publications and *Language Arts*, NCTE.

In *Reading for writing* Janet argues for an approach to reading which is a shared experience, pursued with the support of sympathetic adults. It starts from exposure to stories and rhymes, and only later addresses the components which make up sounds and words – the opposite of the approach required by synthetic phonics.

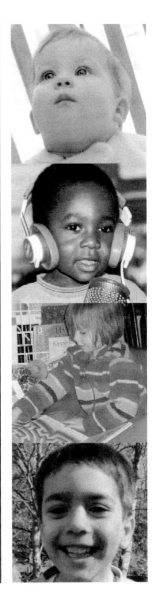

This story, which is called *Rhyming Word Adventures*, uses words that rhyme made into sentences. It was written, illustrated and published by a group of five and six-year-old children. It was a prequel to another slightly more complex book and was linked to work being done in relation to the children's knowledge of letter-onsets and rimes in words, and their ability to make analogies to help them with their reading and writing. The onset is the first consonant(s) in any English syllable and the rime is the rhyming part of words which rhyme. These children were engaged in authentic literacy activities, authoring texts for real audiences to read. Their literacy development was contextualized in meaningful situations, with the phonics element of the work being focused on as just one aspect of a series of multiple, 'self help' strategies which were being used to help them to develop as literacy learners.

> One day a boy called Roy was walking down the road and suddenly he saw ....
> a frog on a dog,
> a fish in a dish,
> ant's in your pant's,
> a man with a pan,
> a fly in a piy,
> a hen on a pen,
> a cat geting a rat,
> a snaike in a lacke.
> At the end of Roy's adventure he went home.
> Did it really hapen or was it his imajinashun.
> The End.

The ongoing debate in relation to how children learn to read has once again reached boiling point with the *Independent Review of the Teaching of Early Reading* (Rose: 2006) which came down heavily in favour of synthetics phonics. Many academics, educators and politicians dispute Rose's conclusions, and the media has had a field day reporting opposing points of view which seem to encompass supporters of synthetic phonics versus people who favour analytic phonics and those who go for a more balanced approach (Cook: 2002).

The ways in which children learn to read and the most effective strategies for teaching reading have always been hotly contested. However, it is crucial to remember that reading is about **making sense of print**; we need to nurture young readers who are capable of making decisions about what they read, when they read and why they read. To enable them to do this they need to know, right from the beginning of their journey to become literate, that books are for pleasure and enjoyment. They make you laugh and cry, they make you angry and sad, they offer information and differing points of view and overall they are worth 'getting to know' because, as Frank Smith (1988) said, we learn from the company we keep (the company of good texts being essential) and by joining the literacy club where children learn 'by participating in literate activities with people who know how and why to do these things'. p7

Making use of multiple cueing systems

Learning to read is a very complex process and there is no single way that works for all children, despite the claims of synthetic aficionados (Johnston & Watson: 2005). As Goodman and Martens (2005) point out,

'Reading is not about decoding or attacking words; it is a process of integrating language cues and strategies with what the reader knows about language and the world to predict and construct meaning across the text.'

If children are taught in phonics dominated classrooms, as opposed to being exposed to a multiplicity of reading cues which they can draw upon to help with their reading development, 'they are in danger of holding their own competence as good readers in low esteem' (Martens: 1996). If in addition to this there is limited exposure to good quality texts and fine literature, then children can easily develop negative attitudes in relation to reading as a process (Meyer: 2002). It is essential that emergent readers are exposed to and encouraged to make full use of all the cueing systems available to them: **semantic** cues concerned with meaning, whether or not a series of words, a phrase or a sentence make sense; **syntactic** cues concerned with grammar, the form and established manner in which words are presented and used in our language; and **graphophonic** cues concerned with letter-sound relationships, the sounds that the letters in the alphabet make and the way in which words are written and spelled.

Children must be shown how to utilize and draw upon these cue systems in the form of self help reading strategies to enable them to become independent readers capable of problem solving as they read. In shared reading situations with authentic, meaningful texts, teachers need to model how to:

- make use of illustrations
- draw on their previous experiences to make sense of the text
- predict what the text might be about
- make good guesses where needed and where appropriate
- read forwards
- read backwards
- look at first letters
- look at last letters
- look at clusters of letters
- draw analogies with patterns of letters in words

- make use of punctuation cues
- see reading as a social process

These are strategies which accomplished readers use naturally and intuitively in their literary activities; however developing readers and writers need help and guidance in their use and adults must constantly model these self help strategies as they read **to** and **with** young children. The aim is that eventually children will be able to draw on the appropriate cues as they read **by themselves** (Mooney: 1990).

It is by looking at how children make use of the differing cueing systems and through analysing their early reading miscues that we see how they attempt to make sense of print. They concentrate not just on letters and clusters of letters, but on constructing meaning from the text. They bring their prior knowledge about print and about their culture to the task of reading, and they constantly monitor their own understanding of a text, back tracking and self correcting if and when needed, and using 'fix-it' strategies where appropriate (Goodman & Marek: 1996).

What kind of phonics should be taught?

It is now widely accepted that the systematic teaching of phonics is an important part of the reading process (Goswami: 2005); it is one of the cueing systems that children need to make reference to as they move towards becoming competent readers. However, with the Rose Report stating that synthetic phonics are to be used first and foremost to teach the basics of reading, a closer look at exactly how English speaking children learn phonics is now necessary. In effect what is currently the issue is not whether phonics should be taught, but what kind of phonics should be taught.

Usha Goswami has carried out extensive research into the way in which young children learn phonics, and has recently been studying the acquisition of reading across the world's languages. She found that 'most children will eventually become competent, indeed skilled readers of their languages, but in some languages this happens much faster than others' (Goswami: 2005, p273). She also noted that phonological awareness develops before literacy development and that this is universal, with all children naturally learning larger units before smaller units; that is, they are aware first of syllables, then of onsets and rimes, and only finally of phonemes - the smallest units of sound that change meaning. The child's natural propensity, therefore, is to learn large, whole units before moving on to the smaller parts. Despite this knowledge, synthetic phonics teaching starts with the smaller units – phonemes. This is an upside down approach, an unnatural, abstract way of learning phonics for the very young child, and especially unsuitable for English speaking children. Goswami pointed out that English is the most

is for Sheep

inconsistent language in the world in terms of the regularity of letter-sound correspondences (with Greek, Finnish, German, Spanish and Italian being the most consistent). Because of this, if English speaking children are taught with only one approach and that approach is synthetic phonics, then we are doing our children a serious injustice and in many cases hindering them from drawing on other cueing systems to aid their reading development. Goswami's research shows that young children initially learn onsets and rimes more easily than phonemes; that is, analytic rather than synthetic phonics.

Goswami notes that there is no ideal way to teach phonics; what matters is that phonics is taught systematically. However, because English has an inconsistent spelling system, we need to develop multiple strategies to help children learn rather than rely on one very rigid approach. Teachers need to understand how the English language system works and how to teach children these multiple strategies. The Rose Report recommends replacing the 'searchlights model', which emphasizes the use of the cueing systems - semantic, syntactic and graphophonic - with just one single strategy; synthetic phonics. This proposal flatly contradicts much research concerning how children learn to read effectively, that is with exposure to a balance of strategies for developing meaning, understanding and enjoyment (Campbell: 1999; Campbell: 2004; Evans:1998; Fox: 1993; Goodman: 1993; Goodman: 1998; Taylor: 1998; Wilson: 2002).

In considering the importance of teaching phonics, Goswami (1999) stated that 'Phonics teaching aims to improve the child's understanding of the relationship between phonemes or groups of phonemes and the letters which make up words or parts of words.' Her later findings are supported by earlier research which showed that the majority of young children find that learning the sounds of individual letters and then blending these sounds to make words is a very difficult, abstract activity which can be meaningless and totally unrelated to the task of learning to read unless they already have an awareness of what reading is all about. She found that children are able to detect phonemes as a result of being able to read; that is, they start to break words up into constituent phonemes after they have started to learn to read. She noted that 'phonemic awareness is a consequence rather than a precursor of being able to read ... rimes are more accessible phonological units than phonemes for young children who are learning to read' Goswami (1995).

Onset - rime analogy

As early as 1986 Goswami discovered that children who are just starting to read make analogies between familiar and unfamiliar written words to decode new, unknown ones (Goswami: 1986). In her work with Peter Bryant (Goswami & Bryant:

1990) she established that children find it much easier to analyse words into onsets and rimes rather than into phonemes, as was originally thought. The onset is the first consonant(s) in any English syllable, which may be single phonemes (e.g. **p**-ig, **j**-og, **d**-oll), double phonemes (e.g. **cr**-ack, **sh**-op, **st**-ep) or treble phonemes (e.g. **str**-ing, **spr**-ing) and the rime is the rhyming part in words which rhyme e.g. p-**ig** and j-**ig**.

Even earlier than this, international research was showing that children have a natural ability to hear onsets and rimes and that they use this ability to make letter-sound correspondences. In other words they can analyse spoken words into onsets and rimes, rather than phonemes, before they begin to read (Wylie and Durrell: 1970; Calfee: 1977; Treiman: 1985).

It was Margaret Moustafa, with her research on whole-to-parts phonics, who moved the onset-rime research on in a way that could be used in the classroom. In studies looking at how children learn to read, Moustafa (1997) concluded that to enable children to pronounce unfamiliar print words we should teach them to make analogies between familiar and unfamiliar print words; we should teach them the sounds of letters that represent onsets and rimes; and we should help them to recognise many print words holistically so they can start to make analogies between known and unknown words. She states that 'the most effective way to help children learn to recognise a lot of print words is to help them read stories with familiar language' (Moustafa, 1998, p18). Young children therefore need exposure to shared reading with a variety of meaningful, patterned, predictable texts.

It is not difficult to find books that contain some of these characteristics. Many traditional nursery rhymes, jingles, poems and picture-story texts have just what is needed. Many settings will have suitable material already, and there are suggestion later in this chapter and elsewhere in this book. Some of the key characteristics which make them easy and pleasurable to recite and remember include the use of rhyming words, repetitive couplets, alliteration, a strong rhythmic quality, predictable texts and an enjoyable, often funny story line which young children clearly relate to.

It is exactly these attributes that make rhymes and jingles such wonderful tutors of young, ready to emerge readers. Iona and Peter Opie (1987), in their comprehensive documentation of children's playground rhymes and jingles, did much to emphasise the importance of exposing young children to nursery rhymes, jingles and songs, while Margaret Meek stated that as well as having an expert reader to model the process of reading, it is also the text that teaches what readers learn (Meek: 1988).

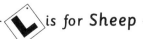

For example, in the following traditional rhyme:

> To market, to market, to buy a fat pig:
> Home again, home again, dancing a jig.
> To market, to market, to buy a fat hog:
> Home again, home again, jiggety-jog.

The words **pig** and **jig** rhyme, as do **hog** and **jog**. Children are able to pick out these rhyming words from the other words and then find more words to rhyme with the rime part of each of them. The teacher can write the rhyming words down in front of the children on a 'word wall' and then add the other words as and when the children say them. In this way a bank of words can be built up which allows children to make links with texts they have read and understood, while at the same time allowing them to make analogies with previously unknown words:

p **ig**	h **og**
j **ig**	j **og**
f **ig**	l **og**
b **ig**	f **og**
d **ig**	d **og**

Whole-to-parts phonics

The way of teaching phonics known as whole-to-parts phonics instruction (Dombey, H., Moustafa, M. et al.: 1998; Moustafa: 1998), makes a great deal of sense and draws upon the knowledge that children make analogies between known and unknown words with the same onsets and/or rimes to pronounce unfamiliar print words. Moustafa (1998, p 19) states that 'whole-to-parts phonics instruction differs from traditional phonics instruction in that (1) it teaches the parts of the words after the story has been read to, with and by children rather than before the story is read by the children, and (2) it teaches letter-onset, letter-rime, and letter-syllable correspondences rather than letter-phoneme correspondences. Yet, like traditional phonics instruction, it is explicit, systematic, and extensive'.

In a careful consideration of phonics teaching, Moustafa (1997) considers that, compared with traditional phonics teaching, whole-to-parts phonics teaching has some significant advantages.

- It is systematic, explicit and extensive
- It is based on recent discoveries in linguistics and psychology
- It goes from whole-to-parts (from whole text, to words, to word parts)
- Instruction occurs after reading (e.g. after a predictable story is read to, with and by children)

- It teaches letter-psychological parts of speech (onset, rime, syllable) correspondences
- It teaches multiple possibilities
- It is contextualized and memorable
- It is psychological, making sense to children learning to read

Before they can start to make analogies to help them read new words it is evident that children need access to many written words which they can recognise. It has already been noted that young children learn to read more effectively from meaningful contexts. Hence their initial forays into reading should be with easy to understand, good quality texts which exhibit a good storyline, a strong sense of rhythm and a lot of rhyming words. The latter will expose them to the written words from which they will start to make analogies to help them with new words. Whole-to-parts phonics is in essence simply going from the whole to the parts; from the known to the unknown; from the concrete to the abstract instead of going the other way round.

Stories - sentences - words - parts of words - working out new words - independent reading

There are many excellent books which emphasise reading as an enjoyable activity, so to move from nursery rhymes and jingles to books with patterned, predictable texts is not difficult. Teachers and adults need to share these books with developing readers as they move from initially needing considerable help from a role model to being able to read by themselves at a later stage. The progression is shown in the diagram below.

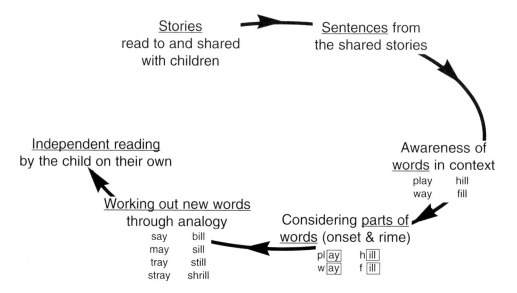

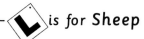
is for Sheep

In her book, *Reading To, With and By Children,* Margaret Mooney outlines how a developing reader moves along a continuum which starts with children being read to **by** an adult. This moves into children reading **with** an adult, finally as children become more confident and competent they start to **read by themselves**, moving to becoming independent readers (Mooney: 1990). Obviously the **to, with** and **by** stages on this continuum very much depend on the types of literature being used and a child's familiarity with the texts.

The "To", "With" and "By" continuum in relation to reading *and* writing

At every stage in a child's journey to be literate, adults need to provide different levels of support depending on the supports and challenges in the texts.

TO	WITH		BY
Reading to Children	Shared Reading	Guided Reading	Independent Reading
Modelled Writing	Shared & Interactive Writing	Guided Writing	Independent Writing

Adapted from Mooney, M. (1990*)* <u>Reading To, With, and By Children</u>
New York, Richard Owen

1. We provide maximum support when we read **to** children. This is usually done where a text provides more challenges than supports and a child couldn't read the text by himself.

2. We provide a great deal of support when we read **with** children. This is where texts have some challenges but also provide a lot of supports and with help children can usually manage to read the text.

3. We provide little or no support when children read **by** themselves. This is where texts have plenty of supports and children can read them independently.

Reading for writing

Working with five and six year old children I found there were many books that they liked and which were excellent examples of meaningful, patterned, predictable texts making good use of rhyming words. A book that children have particularly enjoyed is *Times and Rhymes* (Davidson, 1997), a fine book which uses several different traditional rhymes woven into a narrative about the passage of time and telling the time over the period of one full day. *Times and Rhymes* is almost a puzzle book in that the rhyming couplet plus associated cues on one page encourage the reader to have a guess at what the actual nursery rhyme is on the next page. Using all the cueing systems available to us on each double page spread we started to focus on the overall storyline, reading the book through and talking about the story and the rhymes within the story, the characteristics of the different characters, their behaviour, and the way the story ended. Then we started to look at the words in each of the traditional nursery rhymes. We identified which words rhymed and wrote them down on a 'word wall'. The children's growing awareness of letter - onset and rime - and their ability to make analogies with other similar words led them to question why some words looked the same and sounded the same (**play/way, hill/fill, clock/dock**) and why some words sounded the same and yet were spelt differently (**school/rule, snow/go, see/tea**).

Each Peach Pear Plum (Ahlberg, 1989), *Quick as a Cricket* (Wood, 1994), *This is the Bear* (Hayes, 1986) are other well known books written in rhyming verse. In *Each Peach Pear Plum* the story follows a circular pattern and ends very satisfyingly where it begins. The narrative, which draws on the reader's intertextual knowledge of traditional nursery rhymes, requires its readers to make use of the illustrations and other cueing systems as they attempt to make sense of the print. Despite being a favourite with the children, the rhyming words were not as straightforward in terms of onset and rime and, as with *Times and Rhymes*, the children were obliged to search for words that sounded the same but with different rime spellings as well as ones with the same rime spellings. Once again this was a talking point and quite clearly drew the children's attention to the onset and rime in each word.

Putting the whole-to-parts phonics theory into practice - *Our Little Book of Rhymes*

Working initially as a whole class we started to write down words that rhymed with each other with a view to making an illustrated book of rhyming sentence words. The children noted that many words rhymed and had the same rime spelling, for example, **duck/luck; dog/log; cat/hat; mouse/house; shark/dark**. They also noted that a few words rhymed but had different rime spellings, for example, **beer/ear; bee/tea; John/gone**. It was interesting to note that the children who found it hard to find any words that rhymed were also the children who were experiencing difficulties as emergent readers. This observation tallied with the findings of Bryant et al (1989) who felt that there is a link between a child's early rhyming skills and their eventual progress in reading. As Goswami (1995) stated,

> ...there is a strong and robust connection between rhyming and reading ... children with good rhyming skills make more rime analogies than children

 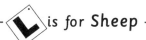

with weaker rhyming skills ... and children with extremely poor rhyming skills do not seem to make rime analogies at all. p70

The resulting book, '*Our Little Book of Riyms*', was made by cutting coloured A4 card in half length ways and binding the pages down the long side on a spiral binder. Each child was given a piece of paper with a small box for the illustration and a longer box for the rhyming sentence. The rhyming sentences were initially written down in rough draft form. Then, as each child was satisfied, they were pasted into the book. The book, which became very popular with the children, was simple, effective and very appropriately illustrated.

A smaller group wrote another rhyming verse book making use of words with the same rime. Almost without knowing it they were being exposed to letter-onset/rime in spelling, and as Moustafa & Franzese (2001) noted

... as instruction in letter – onset/rime analogy in reading begins with reading whole text with familiar language via shared reading, instruction in letter – onset/rime analogy in spelling begins with composing whole, authentic messages via shared writing. p22

The children worked collaboratively on a group book which was made up of individual sentences using words that rhymed. They discussed what would be included and made rough drafts of their initial ideas. The first group book, *Rhyming Word Adventures*, clearly indicated the children's awareness of the language of books and the way in which they are organised.

It was evident that by following this activity the children made a great deal of progress in letter and grapheme recognition, reading and writing. We had begun by looking at rhyming verses, the letter onsets and rimes in rhyming words and forming banks of words on 'word walls', and had finished up with a class book of rhyming sentences and two well thought through group picture books. All had been written enthusiastically, for real audiences for real reasons. We had gone from the whole to the parts and back again to the whole using a variety of meaningful cues with a focus on a strategy for teaching phonics that relates to young children and what they **can** do, not what they cannot do. The work was successful because the children, who were five and six, had reached a stage of linguistic development which enabled them to understand and recognise graphemes, phonemes and rimes. Because of this they learnt quickly.

Conclusion

Children are active constructors of their own learning. When they are provided with situations which make sense, allow them to relate to and draw upon their previous experiences and are engaging, meaningful and enjoyable, then they will be predisposed to learn effectively.

Learning to read is a very complex process and it is unwise to suggest that there is any one best way to teach reading because there simply isn't just one way that works for all children. Reading is the orchestration of a number of different strategies (not just one phonic strategy) hence children being taught via synthetic phonics, one restricted version of one of the cueing systems, in the absence of the other cues, semantic and syntactic, will be at a disadvantage when they come across irregular words that are not decodable. Beginning readers benefit from effective teachers of literacy who understand the reading process, assessment and children themselves (Medwell et al., 1998). Effective teachers integrate aspects of the different cueing systems into their teaching; they use patterned, predictable texts, make use of direct teaching about letter-sound relationships (onset and rimes before phonemes), and help children to spell words through numerous teacher scaffolded interactions. These teachers know that children need to see the results of their efforts and their teaching is subtle, flexible, personalised, learner centred and context aware (Hall, 2006). Hall noted that we need to consider a multiplicity of approaches along with a clear consideration of children's attitudes to reading, their ability to comprehend and the importance of considering home school links. She also stated that good school management with senior managers who respect and understand children is essential, indeed as Dombey (2006) states, 'the most successful schools and teachers focus both on phonics and on the process of making sense of texts'. p6

Synthetic phonics on its own won't provide the answer!

References

Ahlberg, J & A. (1989) Each Peach Pear Plum. Essex, Oliver & Boyd.

Bryant, P. E. et al. (1989) Nursery Rhymes, phonological skills and reading in *Journal of Child Language 16, 407-428, (90).*

Calfee, R. (1977) Assessment of Individual Reading Skills: Basic Research and Practical Applications. in Reber, A.S. & Scarborough, D.L. (eds) *Toward a Psychology of Reading.* New York, Lawrence Erlbaum.

Campbell, R. (2004) Phonics, Naturally: Reading and Writing for Real Purposes. Portsmouth, NH., Heinemann.

Campbell, R. (1999) Literacy from Home to School: reading with Alice. Stafford, Trentham Books.

Cook, M. (2002) (ed) Perspectives on the Teaching and Learning of Phonics. Royston, United Kingdom Reading Association.

Davidson, A. (1997) Times and Rhymes. London, Kingscourt Publishers.

Dombey, H. (2006) How Should We Teach Children to Read? : "Ker" "a" "ter" for "cat" - perfectly straightforward. *Books for Keeps January 2006, No. 156.*

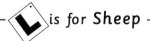 is for **Sheep**

Dombey, H., Moustafa, M. et al. (1998) Whole to Part Phonics: how children learn to read. London, CLPE.

Evans, J. (1998) Reading: Whole to Parts Phonics. *The Primary English Magazine Vol 4, No 1. September/October 1998.*

Evans, J. (ed) (1998) What's in the Picture: responding to illustrations in picture books. London, Sage Publishers.

Fox, M. (1993) Radical Reflections: passionate opinions on teaching, learning and living. New York, Harcourt Brace & Company.

Goodman, K. (1993) Phonics Phacts: A common sense look at the most controversial issue affecting today's classrooms! Portsmouth, NH., Heinemann.

Goodman, K. (ed) (1998) In Defense of Good Teaching: what teachers need to know about the "Reading Wars". York, MN, Stenhouse Publishers.

Goodman, Y. & Marek, A. (1996) Retrospective Miscue Analysis: revaluing readers and reading. New York, Richard Owen Publishers.

Goodman, Y. & Martens, P. (2005) The Influence of Decodable Texts on Readers' Strategies. in Altwerger, B. (ed) (2005) *Reading for Profit: How the Bottom Line Leaves Kids Behind* Portsmouth, NH., Heinemann.

Goswami, U. (1999) Balanced Phonics. A paper for circulation for the Ofsted meeting on 29th March, 1999 on 'The Importance of Phonics in Learning to Read and Write'.

Goswami, U. (1986) Children's Use of Analogy in Learning to Read: a developmental study. *Journal of Experimental Child Psychology No 42, 73-83.*

Goswami, U. (1995) Rhyme in Children's Early Reading in Beard, R. (Ed) (1995) *Rhyme, Reading and Writing* London, Hodder & Stoughton.

Goswami, U. (2005) Synthetic Phonics and Learning to Read: a cross-language perspective in *Educational Psychology in Practice Vol 21, No 4, December 2005, pp. 273-282.*

Goswami, U. & Bryant, P. E. (1990) Phonological Skills and Learning to Read. New Jersey, Lawrence Erlbaum.

Hall, K. (2006) ATC About Phonics? Controversial Issues In Policy, Practice And Research. Keynote speech at conference 'Teaching Reading, Teaching Phonics', Canterbury, 6th January.

Hayes, S. (1986) This is the Bear. London, Walker Books.

Johnston, R. & Watson, J. (2005) The Effects of Synthetic Phonics on Reading and Spelling Attainment; a longitudinal study. Edinburgh, Scottish Executive Education Department. *(see www.scotland.gov.uk/library5/education/sptrs-00.asp).*

Martens, P. (1996) I Already Know How to Read: a child's view of literacy. Portsmouth, NH., Heinemann.

Medwell, J. et al. (1998) Effective Teachers of Literacy. Report of a research project commissioned by the Teacher Training Agency, Exeter, The University of Exeter.

Meek, M. (1988) How Texts Teach What Readers Learn. Stroud, The Thimble Press.

Meyer, R. (2002) Phonics Exposed: understanding and resisting systematic, direct intense phonics instruction. New Jersey, Lawrence Erlbaum Associates.

Mooney, M. (1990) Reading To, With, and By Children. New York, Richard Owen.

Moustafa, M. (1997) Beyond Traditional Phonics: research discoveries and reading instruction. London, Heinemann.

Moustafa, M. (1998) Whole-to-Parts Phonics Instruction in Dombey, H., Moustafa, M. et al (1998) Whole to Part Phonics: How Children Learn to Read. London, CLPE.

Moustafa, M. & Franzese, R. (2001) Do You Hear What I Hear? Helping Children Read, Write And Spell Using Letter–Onset/Rime Analogy in Evans, J. (ed) (2001) The Writing Classroom: Aspects of Writing and the Primary Child 3 – 11. London, David Fulton Publisher.

Opie, I. & Opie, P. (1987) The Lore and Language of Schoolchildren. Oxford, Oxford University Press.

Rose, J. (2006) Independent Review of the Teaching of Early Reading. London, DfES.

Smith, F. (1988) Joining the Literacy Club: further essays into education. Portsmouth, NH., Heinemann.

Taylor, D. (1998) Beginning to Read and the Spin Doctors of Science: The Political Campaign to Change America's Mind About How Children Learn to Read. Illinois, NCTE.

Treiman, R. (1985) Onsets and Rimes as Units of Spoken Syllables: Evidence from Children. Journal of Experimental Child Psychology 39: 161-181.

Wilson, L. (2002) Reading to Live: how to teach reading for today's world. Portsmouth, NH., Heinemann.

Wood, A. 1994) Quick as a Cricket. Singapore, Child's Play International.

Wylie, R.E. & Durrell, D.D. (1970) Teaching Vowels Through Phonograms in Elementary English 47: 787-79.

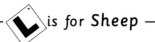

Part 3

How do we put this thinking into practice?

"I hear and I forget. I see and I remember. I do and I understand." Confucius

Part three of this book expands the views, comments and guidance in parts one and two by providing a range of activities for readers to use with children in the Early Years Foundation Stage (particularly in the later stages) and in the early stages of Key Stage 1.

Effective learning in the early years has key features. Young children need movement, repetition, enjoyment and sensory stimulation, and this is enhanced by the sort of 'sustained shared thinking' with adults and peers described in recent research (EPPE Project, DfES: 2004). These features of high quality learning have been recognised in government guidance for the early years. Support for remodelling the primary curriculum suggests that there is now awareness of the continuing need for a practical, integrated curriculum throughout childhood and into early adolescence.

The curriculum for the early years, contained in *Birth to Three Matters*, *The Curriculum Guidance for the Foundation Stage* and the amalgamated Early Years Foundation Stage, is geared to the need for sensory stimulation and active learning during the very early years, but there is an ever present danger that we could be distracted by early goals which expect children to 'sit still and maintain attention' while the curriculum is 'delivered' to them in measured doses and national programmes, or through overly directed, adult planned tasks and activities. The government appears to have taken research on effective learning seriously, but there remains a tension between the need to meet targets and raise standards in simple, numerical terms, and ensuring the quality of experiences for young learners.

In this context it is heartening to read these recommendations within the *Independent Review of the Teaching of Early Reading* (The Rose Report, DfES: 2006) that:

Phonic work for young children should be multi-sensory in order to capture their interest, sustain motivation, and reinforce learning in imaginative and exciting ways.

and

If children are to become successful independent learners, then settings and schools must exploit the conditions that they provide best. The most effective work drew upon all six areas of learning of the Foundation Stage curriculum and experience to fire children's imagination and enrich their communication skills, particularly speaking and listening.

The recommendations contained in any guidance on the development of phonological awareness (the hearing and saying of sounds that make up words) as distinct from phonics (the teaching of the relationship between written spellings and speech sounds) must take into account the findings of recent brain research, the effect of gender on learning, and the effectiveness of different methods of developing such skills. The comparative effectiveness of different methods and the importance of an early start to speaking and listening have been discussed at length earlier in this book. Here we explore some of the research into brain development and some thoughts on the differences in learning between young boys and young girls.

Evidence from brain scans and investigation into the development of young brains gives some clear messages about:

- key features in the development of language
- how hearing develops throughout childhood
- how the young brain receives and interprets sound and words
- differences between the brains of most boys and most girls, and how this may affect the way practitioners proceed.

The development of language and communication has been addressed in previous sections of *L is for Sheep*, where writers have explored the complex and time-consuming business of learning to be an effective talker. All babies and children need to learn how to make and control sounds, and in order to do this each child needs to develop:

- control of the muscles in their mouth, tongue and teeth, achieved not only by making sounds, but by chewing, babbling, sucking, licking and blowing bubbles - in workouts for the mechanics of speech
- an ability to hear and discriminate between human and environmental sounds; this is promoted in situations that are neither too noisy nor too quiet - workouts for the ears and the brain in hearing and copying the sounds that make speech different from other sounds – often referred to as phonological awareness
- a knowledge of how conversations work - the art of taking turns and leaving spaces
- a wide and relevant vocabulary for conversing with others, recounting their experiences, talking themselves through their day, or making stories - the tools of talk
- knowledge of how language works – the wonder of plurals, verbs, names and numbers, questions, imperatives and expletives

 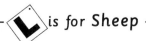

- an understanding of how to use language for different purposes, not just to confirm wants and needs, but increasingly for thinking, imagining, predicting, solving problems and exploring the world.

It is not surprising that most children take between six and eight years to perfect this, so that all the sounds of their own language are distinct. Neurolinguists have now located strong links between brain development, language development, gesture and first hand manipulation of objects, reinforcing the need for a 'hands-on' curriculum for babies and children (Jane Healy).

The first aim of this book is to help practitioners support and enhance the development of phonological awareness, but it is difficult to unscramble the support for this thread of language development from the general tapestry of whole language development. Babies and children don't learn in separate aspects, so we have to recognise that strategies we use will have multiple benefits. In previous chapters, the following needs for children were stressed.

- a world full of **comfortable talk and listening**, attuning babies' and children's ears and brains to the sounds of language
- rich experiences of nursery rhymes, songs and simple poems, fine tuning hearing and speech to the features of **repetition and rhyme**, essential for the generalisation of knowledge in new sounds and words
- frequent **playful exploration of language**, particularly involving and encouraging rhyming, repetition, nonsense and invented words
- **experimenting with the whole range of sounds** of the language or languages they are becoming familiar with, through word play, songs, jingles and tongue twisters
- **using and expanding their vocabularies**, learning and practising new words in conversations, games and role play
- seeing and beginning to **recognise familiar words and letters** and using these in their early mark making and writing
- hearing and seeing **children and adults modelling speaking, listening, reading and writing**, so they can begin to understand the link between them
- handling and enjoying **high quality books** – fiction, non-fiction, poetry and rhyme, often revisiting them over and over again, with adults, with other children and alone
- **multi-sensory learning** where music, singing, movement, sound, rhythm, beat and pattern are all used to enhance their experience.

High quality early years environments are full of these experiences, whether the child is at home, with a childminder, in a nursery or other provision. Talking, listening, and early encouragement to experiment with reading and writing are an accepted part of the planned and informal programme, in both adult directed and child initiated activities. Inventive carers and practitioners provide a rich, stimulating environment, full of opportunities to practise and become confident speakers, attentive and thoughtful listeners, fluent readers and enthusiastic writers. These practitioners are well aware that the development of phonological awareness can only be built on experiences where children are enjoying activities planned for their current stage of development, which take into account their maturity, their interests, their gender and their experiences before, around and during this crucial stage of their development – where children develop 50% of their learning potential (sometimes referred to as their 'intelligence'). High quality settings are alive with the sound of children speaking, listening and thinking, and this is reflected in the recommendations of the Rose Report.

> *The forthcoming Early Years Foundation Stage and the renewed Primary National Strategy Framework for teaching literacy should provide, as a priority, clear guidance on developing children's speaking and listening skills. (Rose: 2006)*

Of course, it is also well known that any provision for young children is rooted in hands-on, practical and physical activity.

> *The richer the sensory environment and the greater our freedom to explore it, the more intricate will be the patterns for learning, thought and creativity. (Hannaford: 1995)*

The reason for this is now proven to be that the part of the brain that processes movement also processes memory and the retention of learning, so action, movement, novelty and engagement will help to reinforce any experience and fix it in the memory. Sensory stimulation also seems to be the key to sparking brain cells into making links and establishing learning. Play has now been recognised as vital in 'fixing' the learning network, strengthening neural pathways so they become permanent features of the child's brain. New learning, stimulated by the rich early years environment, is very fragile until it has been practised again and again in child initiated play.

The key adult role in this process is to provide uninterrupted time and appropriate resources so children can return again and again to activities, practising and refining knowledge, skills and understanding until they become proficient. The results of brain research and the resulting need for a balance of child initiated and adult directed activities is recognised in the Early Years

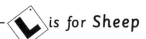
is for Sheep

Foundation Stage (due for implementation in 2008 and building on previous guidance) where such a balanced approach is integral to good practice.

Research into the brains and minds of children also reveals that there are significant differences in the way boys and girls generally process information. Of course it is a mistake to talk about 'all boys' or 'all girls' but there are some general rules, which can help practitioners to ensure that all children succeed.

The first issue is that boys and girls are different. Their brains and bodies develop at different rates, with the result that the readiness of some boys to begin the complex tasks of reading and writing may lag behind the readiness of many girls by some years – in some cases we are asking boys to do things they are not just unwilling, but unable to do.

Boys mature more slowly than girls. A boy's early ease with throwing a ball or climbing may begin with developmental readiness, but his skill and interest grow when he finds interest for his hobby at home. A girl's greater ease with reading and language also appear to begin with an early neurological advantage, enhanced when she is encouraged in her reading habit. The fact that girls mature earlier than boys means that they frequently achieve cognitive milestones at younger ages. (Kindlon & Thompson: 2000)

Another difference between boys and girls is that their brains develop in different ways. The left hemisphere of the brain (the half that deals with language, words, order and sequence) develops more slowly than the right in all children. In boys this development is further delayed by differences in their growth in the womb, and their susceptibility to the hormones which govern both their sex and their gender balance.

Boys (and some girls) may also have more assertive right hemispheres, particularly when they are young. Their interest in large-motor and visual-spatial play activities (climbing, building, manipulating) precedes later maturation of left-hemisphere language centres – and puts many little boys at a disadvantage in school ... (Healy: 1987)

Although at birth boys and girls have about the same numbers of connections between the cells in their brains, most girls are, from a very early age, already using the corpus callosum (the bunch of connective nerve fibres which link the two hemispheres of the brain) to coordinate thoughts and actions in both halves of their brains. This makes it easier for them to organise physical movement and thinking processes between the two different halves of their brains. Combined with a more developed 'locus of control', the earlier development of stereophonic hearing and stereoscopic vision, and faster development of fine motor control, means that many girls have stolen the march on boys in the all important language and reading race before they have even embarked on the formal curriculum in out-of-home care.

Many boys, even at five, are simply not ready for sitting still, for discriminating between the sounds they hear and the letters they see or for beginning the controlled activities of formal phonics teaching. Their strengths are in large motor, visual-spatial activities; they are also risk takers and experimenters, who respond eagerly to solving problems, being active, manipulating materials and equipment, and exploring how things work.

> *There can be little doubt that in terms of literacy, and perhaps all school based education, the most fundamental skill of all is listening. Unless children can discriminate between sounds and listen with growing attention, they will be slow to understand and slow to talk, and here boys can be at a disadvantage. Boys have growth spurts, which can affect their ear canals and lead to significant temporary hearing loss. Often when we think they are not paying attention they actually haven't heard us. Hearing difficulties are more common in boys, and 70 percent of boys of school age have poorer hearing than their female counterparts. This makes it difficult for them to hear sounds and syllables and segment and blend. It can also mean that they experience difficulties in reading and in following instructions. Some six year old children find it hard to understand sentences of more than eight words, so it is really important that practitioners use short sentences and check that children have understood before going on. (Bayley & Featherstone: 2005)*

Remembering this is crucial when planning experiences, games and other activities to reinforce children's growing phonological awareness, and rather than saying 'boys will be boys' we should be working to the strengths and exploiting the abilities of both sexes and the whole gender spectrum by planning a physical, creative and active environment for learning about sounds, using indoor areas and the garden. In this way we will be meeting the needs of all children by adapting the curriculum to the needs of individuals, not implementing a 'one size fits all' programme, which will not work, and may even do long-term damage to children. The implementation of such a formal, centrally imposed programme in the United States has resulted in much criticism and some concern for the long-term wellbeing of children.

> *The serious consequences are yet to be determined as we watch these children during the coming years. Presently, the children's behaviours indicate their responses to the content of the lesson. Finding phonics cognitively and affectively barren, many initiate and communicate (by their actions) a search for stimulation, contact and meaning. They find it in their noses, along their*

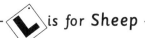

ears, and in their clothing. They find it as they suck a bracelet or touch a friend. Their behaviours communicate the mismatch between learners, curriculum, and the interactions children expect in a social learning setting. The phonics lesson forces kids to have 'tunnel vision' about reading as they focus on sounds rather than read to construct meaning. (Meyer: 2005)

It is essential that practitioners and teachers remember and uphold the sentiments contained in the Rose Report, resisting the pressure to implement inappropriately static, carpet-based programmes just because there is a recommendation to consider 'explicit and well defined' activities. There is no recommendation that the programmes should be organised in formal sessions – 'appropriate formal planning does not underwrite inappropriate formal practice' (Rose). The Report also includes the following suggestions, which preserve the professional judgement of practitioners and teachers:

As children progress, however, some will inevitably learn faster than others. Grouping children for phonic teaching, within an early years setting or class, by matching work to their pace of learning and developing abilities, is often done to good effect. In the best work, too, children are strongly encouraged to help each other, for example, by working in pairs and talking about the task in hand. Again, practitioners and teachers must exercise professional judgments about organising teaching groups to provide optimum conditions for learning. In these respects, good practice in phonic work simply reflects good practice in general.

and

For most children, high quality, systematic phonic work should start by the age of five, taking full account of professional judgments of children's developing abilities and the need to embed this work within a broad and rich curriculum. This should be preceded by pre-reading activities that pave the way for such work to start. (Rose: 2006)

Richard Allington has identified 'Ten Unprofitable but Scientific Strategies for improving reading Achievement', and we have abbreviated them here. They apply to children who have already made a start on the reading and writing journey, so they are perhaps more appropriate to teachers in Reception and Year 1, but they do underline the intertwining links between speaking, listening, reading and writing:

1. Writing, sound stretching and phonemic awareness (early writing is promoted, modelled and demonstrated by teachers, particularly as they speak, articulating sounds clearly and slowly as they write for and with children)

2. Word walls of high frequency words (which scaffold early readers' learning by providing a tool for self monitoring)

3. Just plain writing (better writers read more, and better readers write more)

4. Extended independent reading (good readers develop by reading more!)

5. Discussion after reading (open, sustained, shared thinking, not interrogation)

6. Reading aloud to children (enhanced by open questions, and time for thinking and discussion)

7. Appropriate texts and other fluency enhancing devices (getting really good match between the book and the reader – books that the child can actually read accurately and with comprehension)

8. Choice words (the words teachers use when they read with children – open statements and questions that stimulate thinking, not scripted words from an imposed programme)

9. Motivation (choice from a range of interesting texts, high success, peer interaction)

10. Teacher expertise (not 'one size fits all', centrally directed training, but reflective professional development for individuals and small groups of teachers)

(Allington: 2005)

As in previous sections, we would emphasise that working with children is a sensitive, highly skilled job. Selecting just the right game, activity, song, story or book for the individual or group is not easy and 'best fit' is an aspiration every day! We offer readers the following ideas for activities for your choice and for use within settings. We hope they will form a part of your resource bank of strategies for developing phonological awareness through enjoyable, practical and effective activities for young children.

The contributors to Part Three of *L is For Sheep* are all experts in developing practical activities for young children. Each contributor, or pair of contributors, has concentrated on different materials and situations for developing phonological awareness:

- Helen Bilton offers ideas for thinking abut sounds out of doors
- Penny Tassoni looks at opportunities and ideas for promoting early writing and mark making
- Ros Bayley and Lynn Broadbent contribute activities to encourage movement and dance, and for using toys and puppets

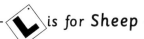 is for **Sheep**

- Kym Scott and Judith Stevens have put together a range of activities, which bring a multi-sensory approach to using objects of all sorts
- Judith Harries explores how sound and music, song and rhyme can enhance your provision.

These activities are all suitable for children in the Foundation Stage (the later stages of The Early Years Foundation Stage) and the early stages of Key Stage 1, and all use familiar and readily available resources. Readers will find reminders of activities already known, simple variations on familiar themes, and new ideas.

Choose the ones which you think will engage the children in your group or setting, and remember that short periods of these activities, combined with a 'rich and varied diet of talking, listening, playing, experimenting, mark making, writing, reading and telling stories' (Rose: 2006) will build phonological awareness in preparation for later stages in the process of becoming readers and writers.

References

Allington, Richard L (2005) <u>Proven Programs, Profits, and Practice: Ten Unprofitable but Scientific Strategies for Improving Reading Achievement</u> in <u>Reading for Profit: How the Bottom Line Leaves Kids Behind</u>, ed. Bess Altwerger, Portsmouth NH, Heinemann

Hannaford, Carla (1995) <u>Smart Moves: why learning is not all in your head</u>. Marshall, NC, Great Ocean Publishers

Healy, Jane M (1987) <u>Your Child's Growing Mind</u>. New York, Broadway Books

Bayley, Ros & Featherstone, Sally (2005) <u>Boys and Girls Come Out to Play</u>. Lutterworth, Featherstone Education

Kindlon, Dan & Thompson, Michael (2000) <u>Raising Cain</u>. New York, Random House

Meyer, Richard J (2005) <u>Invisible Teacher/Invisible Children: The Company Line</u> in <u>Reading for Profit: How the Bottom Line Leaves Kids Behind</u>, ed. Bess Altwerger, Portsmouth NH, Heinemann

Rose, Jim (2006) <u>Independent Review of the teaching of Early Reading: final report</u>. London, DfES

L is for Sheep

Helen Bilton
Miss, I want that bike

Helen Bilton is an independent consultant who specialises in the development and education of children in the early years.

Helen is a trained nursery/infant teacher and has a particular interest in outdoor play. She was very fortunate to be tutored at university by a nursery garden expert, and this led to a realisation of how the outdoor environment can contribute to children's learning and a continuing passion for working with children outside. She has published a number of books on outdoor play, including *Outdoor Play in the Early Years: Management and Innovation* (David Fulton, 2002), *Playing Outside: Activites, Ideas and Innovation for the Early Years* (David Fulton, 2004) and most recently *Learning Outdoors: Improving the Quality of Children's Play Outdoors* (David Fulton, 2005), a handbook for outdoor play written with early years advisers from The London Borough of Brent.

Helen runs a range of training courses on outdoor play and provision across the UK, and provides training in the environment for learning, assessment and observation, boys' and girls' education, and questioning and explaining. At Reading University she contributes to various early years courses.

In *Miss, I want that bike* Helen begins by outlining the importance of outdoor play and the huge contribution it can make to creating a rich language environment for the child, before going on to suggest and describe activities to promote and stimulate the use of language and to help children prepare for reading.

Imagine this scene. The adult is scanning the playground. It is alive with the noise and movement of children running, shouting, shrieking, playing. She spies John, momentarily stationary.

'Err,' the adult says, 'John, can you get off the bike and let Ben have a turn?'

John doesn't look happy, but he rides over slowly, gets off the bike grudgingly and plods off without a bye your leave.

'There you go' says the adult, gesturing toward the bike. Ben jumps on and peddles off. The adult looks at her watch and is glad there's only another five minutes left.

This can be the level of conversation in the average nursery play area, and it's a waste! This type of exchange, sadly all too common in many early years environments, misses a host of opportunities for developing phonics out of doors. The typical approach to outdoor play is often to treat it simply as a chance for children to let off steam; and of course, all children need opportunities to run and shout, flex themselves physically and burn off their boundless energy. But to see the outdoor space as simply for this is to ignore some wonderful opportunities for using the outdoor environment to stimulate and enrich learning. So this section of *L is for Sheep* is about developing phonics out of doors.

The first, and obvious, step is the creation of a language environment. That is, an environment where children are able to hold real and meaningful conversations with each other and with adults.

To create an effective outdoor language environment requires a genuine commitment to the principle that the space outside the setting is an invaluable learning resource, as important in its way as the space inside. In a nutshell, what practitioners need to do is view the outside as half of a whole. Inside is one half and outside is one half; together they make the whole. What follows from this is that outside should receive planning attention, resources, equipment and adult input on the same level with that devoted to the inside. Just as the indoor space needs to be demarcated and planned to provide different areas for learning, so the spaces outside need to be organised to provide activity areas, and the potential of each of these should be examined to see how it can contribute to the use and development of language. It will be useful to consider how and where to cater for the following.

- imaginative play
- building and construction
- gymnasium (climbing)
- small motor skills

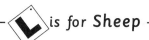
is for **Sheep**

- gardening
- science and environmental activities
- art and making things
- quiet activities.

In the cases of some of the above it is easy to see how they can play a part in promoting language development (e.g. imaginative play); for others the potential is less clear. Nevertheless, it is there, and our task as practitioners is to be aware of how we can create opportunities for children to communicate in all of them. It is hoped that the activities suggested later in this section will provide some ideas.

These outdoor areas have to be resourced, and adults need to be available to work with children and support their play. What is wonderful about the opportunities offered outside is the space and freedom available. Outdoor spaces have characteristics that are special, and different from what can be offered inside. Outdoors many children are able to exult in a confidence in their physical abilities, and do not feel the inhibitions they may experience indoors, either in the setting or at home. Children tend to feel that in a secure outdoor space it is they who are in control, not the adults. So children can often find learning outside much easier than in.

The freedom and space of outdoors offer opportunities for different approaches to learning, whether it be learning language or anything else. Spoken language can be developed through and alongside the movement that comes so naturally out of doors. We have a rich heritage of playground games. Children have made up rhymes to go along with skipping, ball games, and the like for many years. It is almost as though children intuitively know that movement and language go hand in hand. In these games they play with words to understand the sounds and rhythms. They are also enjoying the word games, and children really do need to enjoy words to want to end up reading and writing them! This is what we need to see as the essence of outdoor play – somewhere words and sounds can be played with and enjoyed in a variety of contexts which absorb both the child's imagination and physical energy. Phonics outside is about focusing on the sound of words and letters and phonemes and the link with the correct grapheme, on the rhyme of words, and on moving to syllabic rhythms. Children need to learn to hear the phonemes in speech before they can relate them to print, so the more they experiment with sounds through play, the better.

There are many games and activities suitable for outside, and I suggest some below. Often the most successful follow traditional lines - skipping, ball games, follow my leader, chalking games. Some of the examples may seem quite difficult, but what makes one child sparkle may not interest another. Therefore children need to be challenged, and introduced to a wide range of sounds and rhyming words. In most cases we need to offer these activities repeatedly, until children thoroughly understand an activity's requirements and become accomplished in meeting its demands. For example, many young children, when asked what rhymes with cat, will say 'dog'. Practitioners and adult supporters need to be prepared for answers such as this, and to realise that children need time and practice to understand what 'rhyme' means, and then to respond.

The aim of the activities which follow is to encourage children to use language. We adults are still too often guilty of talking too much and not listening enough. In these activities it is the child who should be talking, not the adult, and they should be planned and organised so that real talk happens. The most effective – but not the only – focus for this is imaginative play. Children need opportunities to play out a visit to, for example, a post office. They need the adults to support and enable them in this – collecting and making resources, modelling possible scenes and situations in a post office (without interfering in the free flow of children's play) – so that when the role play area is set up the children have lots of stimuli and plenty of ideas to use. Adults can then add to the repertoire of ideas as the days unfold.

Equipment and resources help, but children can manage with remarkably little. Something as simple as a large cardboard box can be a shelter, a space ship, a car, a ticket office. A blanket thrown across two chairs can be a cave, a tent, a lair. Bikes are wonderful resources because they add movement. They can be so many things, and if they are available in a setting they can be incorporated into imaginative play by becoming pizza delivery bikes, fire engines, police cars, dispatch riders, ice cream vans, or simply the family car on a day's outing. Making sure that the planning and preparation have been done meticulously will mean that the children have a rich fount of ideas from which to draw, enabling them to create in their imaginations worlds and scenes which will provide contexts for practising and developing their emerging language.

Experience of and familiarity with traditional games and imaginative play are beneficial to children in their early years and will help them in the future, giving them a strong repertoire of games to use when they leave their early years settings and move on to the primary playground, where more often than not they will be left to their own devices.

is for **Sheep**

Skipping rhymes

You can make these up instantly, using familiar words, words from a topic, new vocabulary, or the sounds you are focusing on at the moment - for example:

P, p, party, p, p, pig, p, p, pansy, p, p, pin
S, s, sandy, s, s, sea, s, s, starfish, s, s, sun
Ch, ch, ch, ch, Charley and the Chocolate Factory
F, f, f, f five fat frogs
S, s, s, s, seven snakes slithered around the swamp
Th, th, th, th thirty thin thistles
M for minibeasts, s for snail, b for beetle, all in a pail
Stegosaurus in a swamp, Pterodactyl up a tree, Diplodocus in a lake, can't catch me!

Use popular songs and familiar names - an old version:

Mickey Mouse came to my house,
I asked him what he wanted.
He stamped his foot
And broke a cup
And that is what he wanted

a new version:

Superman, Batman, superheroes all
Cat Girl, Bat Girl, we can be them all
Flying high, being brave
Swooping, flying, lives to save.

Under fives
<u>can</u> skip - they just
need to be shown and to
be enthused to do it!
Soft, light ropes of the right
length are essential to
success. Use these rhymes
for hopping, jumping or
stamping too.

Alphabet practice rhymes for skipping, stamping or jumping

A, B, C and vegetable goop, What will I find, in my alphabet soup? A, B, C, D, E, F, G, H, I, J, K, L, M, N, O, P, Q, R, S, T, U, V, W, X, Y, Z

Or days of the week

Apples, peaches, pears and plums, Tell me when your birthday comes, January, February, March, April, May, June, July, August, September, October, November, December.

For rhyming practice:

Hop, hop, hop
Pop, pop, pop
Stop, stop, stop
Before you drop.

OR

Skip, trip, slip, dip
Stamp, tramp, damp, lamp
Hop, pop, drop, cop
Lump, dump, hump, pump
Keep on hopping, do not stop.

Another old favourite brought up to date:

Each, peach, pear, plum, I spy Tom Thumb
Tom Thumb in the wood, I spy Robin Hood
Robin Hood in the cellar, I spy Cinderella
Cinderella at the ball, I spy Mr Small
Mr Small at his house, I spy Mickey Mouse
Mickey Mouse getting hotter, I spy Harry Potter.
Harry Potter is a star, S-T-A-R

Ball games

Roll or toss a ball from one to another in pairs as you say words starting with the same letter or sound.

Toss a ball or bean bag from hand to hand as you repeat rhyming words such as bat, hat, cat, fat, mat, rat etc.

Roll the ball and keep a sound going until the ball stops - oooooo, eeeeeee, aaaaah, aaaaaay or with cvc words such as kit/kat, kit/kat, kit/kat, kit/kat or dig/dog, dig/dog, dig/dog, dig/dog, dig/dog.

Follow my leader

The leader chooses an action and repeats the word -
j, j, j, jump
h, h, h, hop
sk, sk, sk, skip
st, st, st, stamp.

Follow a line

Draw some wiggly lines, spirals or stepping stones on the ground with chalk or paint. Children follow the lines while chanting sounds, names, nonsense rhymes or rhyming words -

sh, sh, sh, sh, sh, sh

tim/tam, tim/tam, tim/tam, tim/tam, tim/tam

wiggly worm, wiggly worm, wiggly worm

patty pan, patty pan, patty pan, patty pan

jam for Jim, jam for Jim, jam for Jim

Peter painter, Peter painter, Peter painter

pizza pie and peppermint, pizza pie and peppermint

taradiddle Tony, taradiddle Tony, taradiddle Tony

Sarah, Susan, Sally-ann, Sarah, Susan, Sally-ann

Martin, Michael, Mumtaz, Miriam

Hoops

Swing a hoop while saying a long sound -

sh, sh, sh, sh
oo, oo, oo, oo
ee, ee, ee, ee
ay, ay, ay, ay
ing, ing, ing, ing

Using instruments outside

Use all sorts of home made and found instruments to encourage singing, chanting and movement out of doors.

Sticks for tapping, ribbon sticks, shakers, drums, wood blocks, cutlery and metal pans etc all help chidlren to practice their listening skills and sense of rhythm and beat.

You could also use a portable CD player or tape recorder with favourite songs to accompany or encourage karaoke!

These games all need an adult to start them off, but children will soon start using them independently and making up their own versions.

Use the weather

Stamp in puddles, squish the mud, feel the raindrops, watch the clouds. These are all opportunities for children to expand their vocabularies and use new words as they move freely out of doors.

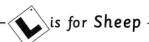
is for Sheep

Use all the familiar activities that children love, to support language development, listening, exploration of words and sounds.

Sand and water

Build up your own stock of words and actions to reinforce descriptive vocabulary and sounds in these familiar activities:

spray, splash, splat, spread, spill

drip, dribble, droplet, dropping.

Collect words to describe water and sand:

bob, bump, bubble, ripple, wavy, trickle, spring, gritty, crumply, damp, moist, squishy, soggy, squelchy, fragile, dusty, silky, solid, smooth, shiny, wavy, scratchy.

Children can add to this list when they know it exists, and older chidlren will begin to use it in their composing and descriptive writing.

Imaginative and role play

Make sure that role play is part of your planning for outdoors, and always give children opportunities to talk, listen, read and write as they play in role. Children need to learn the specialist language for their specialist play - the language of:

the ice cream van
the pizza delivery
the decorators
the window cleaner
the shop
the hospital
the petrol station
the removal company
the garage mechanics
the car wash
the postal sorting office
the newsagent

Spend time with groups looking at books, reading and creating stories, sharing poems and singing songs, so they have the words they need to realise their play.

Words for movement (acknowledgements to Homerton College PE Department)

whirl	gather	whip	twirl	close
twist	run	plunge	press	open
shrink,	scatter	zigzag	push	flutter
slither	dash	tremble	tiptoe	encircle
turn	crumple	skim	creep	hover
glide	soar	throw	collapse	arch
leap	drag	rock	expand	wander
bound	settle	hop	clap	sway
shatter	pause	skip	rise	
spin	crouch	wander	fall	
crawl	burst	toss	shrivel	

Weave and tie, spray and paint

Small movements are important too, because they encourage left/right brain links. Try:

- weaving in fences and garden netting
- tying with ribbon and string
- painting with water
- spraying with water or dilute paint
- chalk and crayons in both hands on big paper
- painting with two brushes
- joining found materials with tape and clips
- washing clothes and hanging them up
- using squeegees and scrapers
- mark making on clipboards and white boards
- throw bean bags in buckets, roll balls down tubes and guttering

Keep moving

Movement helps learning. Encourage all chidlren, both boys and girls to get involved in all sorts of activities. If you make movement fun, they will join you. Suggest ring games, ball games, singing and action rhymes. Do this informally with small groups, rather than having adult directed, whole group sessions.

Start things off - Simon Says, What's the Time Mr Wolf, Hopscotch, chalk games and just let the children join in. Always offer balls, beanbags, hoops and other small apparatus as well as wheeled toys and footballs. Model how to use these in traditional games as well as simple fun and invention.

Listen!

Spend time really listening out of doors - help children to hear small sounds of nature, bees, birds, leaves as well as the sounds of traffic.

Listen for the wind, the rain, water in gutters and drips from trees.

hear the distant sounds of planes and fire engines, church bells and car alarms.

and some inside things outside

Some activities that we naturally think of as indoor ones are great for developing speaking, listening, reading and writing out of doors.

Try some of these:

- a book basket and a rug
- a tape recorder
- an alphabet mat and objects
- sound lotto on carpet tiles
- phonic baskets of objects
- magnetic/wooden letters
- a flip chart
- puppets and soft toys
- a basket of instruments
- a sound tape
- blackboards and white boards
- computer games
- word walls

Make sure the adults make a difference to play and movement out of doors. Don't just stand there, keep moving!

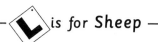 is for **Sheep**

Penny Tassoni
Writing and mark making

Penny Tassoni is an education consultant, author and trainer, who trained and worked as an early years and primary school teacher before becoming a college lecturer. She specialises in the whole spectrum of early learning and play.

Penny has written nineteen books, including the best selling 'Planning Play and the Early Years' (Heinemann, 2005). She also writes for several magazines, including features for parents. Penny is an experienced trainer and her workshops feature at the Primary and Early Years exhibitions in both London and Manchester, as well as in the professional development programmes of many local authorities. In addition to training, Penny works as a reviser for CACHE, the awarding body for childcare, education and playwork qualifications in the U.K. She has worked as a consultant and key note speaker in Istanbul and Japan. Penny is Chair of A2P, a charity whose aim is to educate teenagers about the realities of having a baby.

In *Writing and mark making* Penny looks at some of the factors involved in the child's development of writing skills. She distinguishes between writing and handwriting before briefly reviewing the importance of hand preference and the place of gross and fine motor development. She offers advice on encouraging the child's sensitivity to the sounds and shapes of letters and goes on to emphasise the importance of modelling writing, especially for boys. Her section concludes with suggestions and ideas for activities to put her recommendations into practice.

W riting is a wonderful process! Moving words in your head onto paper or a screen for others to see is empowering. Sadly though, many children are put off writing before they even have a chance to get going and discover this pleasure. This section looks at how we might help children to become confident writers and suggests activities that should support and extend their learning. But first let us look at some of the factors involved in writing.

Handwriting and writing

The starting point when talking about writing is to make a distinction between *writing* and *handwriting*. Writing is the process of finding words, while handwriting is the tool by which we may put them onto paper. Too often in children's early days of writing, the focus is all on handwriting and spelling. This emphasis can lead young children to lose confidence and to use only those words that they know they can form correctly. This can lead to 'safe' writers in Key Stages 1 and 2, or children who spend most of their time asking for help with spellings.

Encouraging handwriting

While the emphasis when children write should be on the meaning of their words, handwriting is nevertheless an important tool that children need to master. Handwriting is about the control of children's hand-eye co-ordination and fine motor movements.

Hand preference

It is desirable for children to develop a strong hand preference. Children who do not have a strong hand preference are more likely to struggle with the process of learning to read. This goes back to brain development (see p101). Handedness is thought to be decided before birth, perhaps even at the moment of conception, and so whilst we cannot determine a child's handedness, we can strengthen it. Activities that require one hand to stabilise and the other hand to be 'active' are useful in this respect. Traditionally children practised these movements by being given everyday tasks around the home. By replicating these activities and adding some similar ones into your everyday routines, you can help children not only to gain skills of self-reliance, but also to improve their fine motor movement. There is a list of suggestions below. Improving children's co-ordination of both hands also helps them as they write. One hand should be steadying the paper, while the other one is engaged in writing. You can encourage this by offering activities such as...

cutting fruit, e.g. bananas
spreading butter or paste onto bread
pouring a glass of water using both hands
washing and drying up beakers

hanging coats onto coat hangers

threading beads onto a lace.

In all these activities one hand is stabilising (the banana, the bread, the glass) while the other is active (cutting, spreading, operating the tap).

Gross motor development

Most other countries do not encourage formal writing until children are around six or seven years old. This is because they recognise that children's overall fine motor skills are not likely to be sufficiently developed and also because they realise that children are able to process symbols more effectively from around six years. In the United Kingdom we are required to start a child's formal education earlier, but it is worth replicating some of the techniques that are used abroad. The key to good handwriting is early gross motor development. By gaining a fluidity of movement in the arms, children are able to control their fine motor movements more effectively. We can also combine this with the process of helping children to use their bodies to explore letters, 'feeling' their shapes. It is also useful to make sure children are given plenty of opportunities for large scale mark making. Big is beautiful when it comes to early handwriting, as large size encourages children to retain fluidity while gaining control of their movements. This is essential for later cursive handwriting.

Fine motor development

Fine motor skills and hand-eye co-ordination are the other essential ingredients for fluid handwriting. Children need plenty of opportunities to use their hands during play. It is important to stress here that we need to check that we are providing sufficient challenge, in order to extend the accuracy of the child's hand movements. This may mean employing strategies such as putting some tiny bottles into the water tray and seeing if the child can pour water into them accurately, or putting some large spoons in the sand tray to see if the child can use them to fill up a smallish container. In the same way, we need also to provide hand strengthening activities, such as squeezing water from sponges into a container or putting out a tray of bottles with lids on and seeing whether children can untwist them.

Supporting early letter formation

Two movements are useful for children to acquire as they mark make. First of all, children need to make anti-clockwise rotational movements starting at the top. This movement forms the starting point for many of the circular letters in the Roman alphabet such as the **a**, **c**, **d** and even **s**. The second movement that is needed is a vertical stroke that begins at the top. This is the starting point for letters such as the **b**, **t**, and **h**. If children have acquired these movements, many of the problems of later incorrect letter formation are avoided because they almost instinctively have a 'feel' for how to present these shapes. It is worth beginning by assessing which children have already acquired these marks. This can be done by simply putting out a sensory material, for example sand, and asking individual children if they can make their finger 'go round the roundabout.' Watch then to see where children start and the direction in which they make the circle. For the vertical movement, ask children to 'stroke' the sand. Once you know which children need further support to acquire these movements, plan some sensory activities that will help them – e.g. making roundabouts in shaving foam, or taking a toy car around a race track of dry rice.

Enjoying the sounds of the words

As well as working on children's handwriting skills, we need also to give children opportunities to mark make and write 'their' words. At first we may see rotational marks and then the addition of vertical marks. Gradually, symbols appear that look increasingly similar to the letters in the child's name. A child's name is often the first word he writes. This is because children's names have a unique meaning for them and they are often exposed to them. Look out for children who are beginning to draw representationally, but choose on occasion to 'write'. Listen, too, for children who mark-make and narrate at the same time. Talking and mark making should go together, as eventually we need children to associate making marks with 'getting down' the words that they are saying or hearing in their heads.

Drawing children's attention to letter shapes and sounds

If we want children to enjoy the activity of writing, it needs not only to be meaningful but also a sensation they find pleasurable. Providing wonderful pens, chalks and paint can make the actual movements enjoyable and so encourage mark making, but to make it meaningful we need to draw children's attention to letter shapes and sounds. Their name is a fantastic starting point, as are labels in the environment. The role of the adult here is to draw attention to the symbols and to use key words such as names as often as possible. We might, for example, have a signing-in register where children have a go at making their mark alongside their name.

Role Modelling

Finally, everyone knows that children are hugely influenced by adults' behaviour. They learn from what they see and often imitate the same behaviours. This happens even when the adult is not intentionally trying to teach the child!

 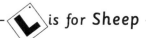

When it comes to writing, we need to capitalise upon this influence. Children should see that adults write, and that writing is something that is important and valued. This is particularly relevant today as there are fewer everyday opportunities for children to see writing in the home and out and about. People no longer write cheques when shopping, waitresses rarely take orders with a pen and pad and doctors often type out prescriptions. Much of the writing that before was done by hand is now done on machines. The type of writing that children do see adults engaged in is often of short duration and usually done perching or standing up; e.g. a quick shopping list done at the breakfast bar or a signature done at the counter of the post office. This must have an impact on the view that children take of writing. It is no wonder that some children do not want to sit down and write, because this is not something that they have seen the adults in their lives do and therefore it can't be important.

It is essential that we role model writing, and work to create an interest in it. This we can do by taking the time to sit down and to write ourselves. Interestingly, we do not even need to ask children to watch us. Quite often, children will gather around an adult who is obviously engaged in something of 'adult importance' and then ask the adult what she is doing. The key is often to carry on writing but to casually invite children to try it for themselves. It is also useful to narrate aloud what you are doing, but in a way that sounds like you are mumbling to yourself. In this way, we draw children's attention to the shape and sounds of some key letters. It is also worth writing in a slow but deliberate way. This allows children to see (and hear) correct letter formation. Learning alongside adults as they engaged in a task was, of course, a traditional way by which children all over the word gained skills and knowledge. In using it to teach children to write, we are just replicating a fairly natural process.

Boys and writing: a footnote

Some boys do not regard writing as a 'male' activity, because it is not something they see the men in their lives do. Boys in particular need to see men and older boys engaged in the process of writing, but it is important for girls to see this too. Both boys and girls are noticing gender activities and are beginning the process of gender identification, and so it is essential that they see writing as an appropriate activity for both sexes. This may mean getting students, dads and male staff to come into the setting to model writing in the presence of the children, at a writing table or using writing alongside other play activities.

The Letter Board

This is a variation on having a post box. The letter board is simply a board where children can pin up their drawings and writing. They can also post notes to each other by writing each others' names or finding a child's name card.

Dedicate a display board for this activity. Put a title up such as 'Our Letter Board' and place tinsel around the edges. There is something about tinsel that makes children feel that this must be a special and fun place for their letters. Prepare a table nearby with drawing and writing materials. Make sure that there is a rich source of lovely paper, pens, envelopes and stamps, as well as office items such as paper clips, staplers and Post-it notes. Begin by telling children that if they have a letter, drawing or note that they wish to give someone, including their parents, they can pin it on the letter board. Show them how to find another child's name and encourage them to come for help.

Get the ball rolling by writing your own letter for another member of staff and putting it up on the wall.

Resources

tinsel for border
writing pads, envelopes
other types of office paper for the table
pens, pencils, crayons and other mark makers
scissors, sticky tape, stamps and paper clips
names of children in the setting
key adult names
Blu-tac for putting up children's letters

Variation

Look out for a metal surface so that children can use fridge magnets to post up their letters.

Create an outdoor area for writing and a special area to put notes such as a hollow in a tree or put up a small wooden box.

What does the adult do?

Adults need to use this table and board to stimulate children's interest, and role modelling is a key way in which we can help children to learn about writing. Adults may also need to be on hand to help children address their envelopes.

Do's and don'ts

Do prioritise taking time to sit and write yourself.

Do draw children's attention to letter shapes as you are writing.

Don't correct children's writing.

Don't worry if some children prefer to draw.

Extensions and observation

Create a mini-postal system. Give children tokens or coins to pay for stamps before they can put them on the board. Designate children as postal workers and even provide them with a uniform!

Observation

Note the letter shapes that children are using.

Keep a note of children who enjoy this activity.

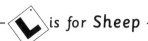

A Painting Wall

This is a wonderful activity that encourages mark making and has the added advantage of developing children's creativity.

The idea of a painting wall is that children can paint on a large scale and thus develop the gross motor movements that act as a precursor for the finer movements required for fluent handwriting. It is a 'must' for every early years setting.

This activity has many fantastic spin offs. Firstly, by using a palette approach to painting, children learn about colour mixing for themselves. It also means the end of cleaning paint pots for you, as children learn to wash up for themselves.

Resources

plastic sheeting or shower curtains
masking tape
rolls or sheets of paper
small polystyrene trays such as apple trays
ready mixed paint in primary colours (red, yellow, blue) and white
large brushes - buy cheap packets of decorators' brushes from a local 'pound shop'
cleaning-up cloths

Variation

Children can paint over your marks with a different colour so they can see colours mixing.

Find the largest stretch of wall, window or cupboard space you can, indoors or outside. Protect inside walls by lining with a shower curtain or thick plastic secured with masking tape. Put up sheets of continuous paper, held up again with masking tape, or use a roll of paper. If necessary protect carpeted areas with a strip of non-slip plastic carpet protector available at most carpet shops and DIY centres.

Give each child a small plastic or polystyrene tray with a blob of each of the primary colours of paint, some white paint and a large paint brush. Encourage the children to make marks or to paint freely. When children have finished, ask them to put their tray under the running water and to use the brush to wipe it clean.

What does the adult do?

You could simply act as a facilitator and encourage the child to enjoy painting on a large scale. For a more structured activity focusing on letter shapes, you could play a 'follow my leader' game. Take a brush and model the letter shape and then move aside for the children to make the same letter shape in a space nearby. The wall is an ideal place to help very young children to make anti-clockwise rotational movements and vertical marks beginning at the top. You can also work with individual children and show them how to make the letters in their name.

Do's and don'ts

Don't keep this activity for special occasions. Children need large scale all the time.

Do make sure that you take the time to paint as well - role modelling is a powerful tool.

Do use this as an enjoyable way to show children how to form letters correctly.

Observation

Look out for children who find it hard to co-ordinate their movements.

Observe whether children have a preferred hand.

Moving Marks to Music

This is a simple activity designed to appeal to a wide age range of children. It is specially useful for helping an older child who has lost confidence in their writing skills. It is also an excellent way of promoting hand-eye co-ordination and relaxing children's wrists.

This should be a pleasant sensory experience for children and one that they will want to return to regularly. It is also a group activity so that children can enjoy mark making together with their friends.

Resources

large sheets of paper to cover a table

masking tape

some smoothly rhythmical music

chubby crayons

pens and different sized markers

pastels

Stretch out a large sheet of paper so that it covers an entire table.
Put out markers or pens and put on some music. Encourage children to come and make marks to the music. Can they take their pens or crayons for a walk?

What does the adult do?

The adult can either act as a facilitator by providing the materials and encouraging children or better still, sit with the children and model marks and patterns. The latter role encourages reluctant writers and stimulates interests in the activity.

Try and encourage children not to be territorial over the paper. This is a good co-operative group activity. If there is a problem, divide the paper using pen line boundaries.

Do's and don'ts

- Do sit with children and enjoy the experience of marking
- Do make this a judgement- free activity - so don't correct pencil grip or make comments on their work.

Variation

Secure the paper on a vertical surface and use paint (see The Painting Wall) or go outside using chalks on walls. Consider changing the marking implements to create interest.
Put out ribbons, sequins, tinsel and other interesting materials so that children can enjoy coming back to the activity.

Variation

When the chidlren have finished the activity, use the paper as a background for collage or for a display.

Observation

Have children established hand preference yet?

Are children making anti-clockwise rotational movements? Do they make vertical marks starting at the top?

Are children relaxed in this activity - look at the non-writing hand and check this is not clenched.

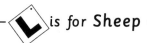

is for Sheep

Nibbles the Writing Mouse

Nibbles is a small, white, puppet mouse that sparks an interest in writing.

This activity helps children to see and enjoy the process of writing as a tool for communication. It is a wonderfully flexible activity that can be adapted to meet the reading and writing levels of individual children.

Find a puppet or soft toy that you can 'bond' with (it doesn't **have** to be a mouse!).

Introduce the puppet to the children. Tell the children that the puppet's mum or dad wants to know what the children and the puppet have been doing. Suggest that if the children have time, maybe they could write a note or draw a picture for the puppet's mum or dad.

Put out a box or bag on the writing table so that children can post their notes. Once a child writes a note and puts it in the box, write a quick reply from the fictitious mum or dad. Keep the note short and use key words that you wish children to pick up on. Eight or ten words is often enough!

Give the note to the child. At the start of the activity do this in a loud voice so that other children learn that if they write a note, they will get a response. Keep the format of letters the same for children who are not yet reading. Over several letters, children will develop word recognition. Use alliteration to draw children's attention to sounds in words.

Try to make this a regular activity.

What does the adult do?

You need to watch this activity and note who is at the writing table in order to reply. To get the activity off to a flying start, you could model writing a letter.

Avoid making this a directed activity. Children generally come because they see that other children have got reply letters. This is also a lovely activity for parent helpers or students to be responsible for. While the children are writing, adults must refrain from commenting about how and what they write. This activity is a non-judgement zone!

Do's and don'ts

Do frame a reply as soon as possible.

Do keep letters short and matched to children's reading level.

Don't interfere with children as they are writing.

Do offer this activity frequently.

Resources

puppet or soft toy

paper and envelopes

an assortment of pens

box for posting letters

Variation

Use a variety of different characters for children to write to - perhaps an outdoor wizard who hides his replies in the fence

Extension

Base the content of the reply letter on the letter shapes and sounds that you wish to draw the children's attention to.

Observation

See whether the quantity of writing increases in response to a 'non-judgemental' writing context.

Notice whether children are using their reply letters in order to write.

L is for Sheep

Ros Bayley & Lynn Broadbent
Tune into sound as you move around

Following an extensive career as an early years teacher, Ros Bayley now works as a consultant, trainer and storyteller. She has always had a keen interest in the teaching of literacy and has written many publications for early years professionals, including *Foundations for Independence* (2nd edition 2005), *We Can Do It!* (2004), *Boys and Girls Come Out to Play* (2005) and *Smooth Transitions* (2003), all collaborations with Sally Featherstone and published by Featherstone Education. She is co-author (with Sue Palmer) of *Foundations of Literacy* (Network Continuum, 2004). Ros really enjoys writing with other professionals and has written a number of books with Lynn Broadbent (published by Lawrence Educational Publications).

Lynn Broadbent is an early years adviser with extensive experience of teaching and working with practitioners. She has co-written a number of books, which include *Flying Start With Literacy* (Network Continuum, 2005) and *Helping Young Children To Listen* (Lawrence Educational Publications, 2001). She has a keen interest in the teaching of literacy in the early years and has developed, alongside Ros Bayley, a wide variety of resources to assist professionals in this important work.

In *Tune into sound as you move around* Ros and Lynn argue for the importance of movement in helping learning. They describe the key part played by the development of a steady beat and a sense of rhythm, and how these skills contribute to preparation for reading. The activities which follow show how their ideas can be put into practice.

Movement is indispensable to learning! When we move we activate our brains, and in consequence process information more effectively. When the body is engaged, so is the mind, and this is particularly true for young children. They relish movement and are rarely still, so much so that we are often left enviously wondering where all that energy comes from!

All early year's educators understand the value of movement. When children become restless the first thing we do is get them moving. 'Show me your fingers' we intuitively announce. This is usually followed by a vigorous display of 'Heads, shoulders knees and toes,' or 'Simon says,' after which, and as if by magic, the children find it easy to re-focus! We have always known that movement is essential to learning, and now this intuitive understanding is supported by research. Data from studies of anatomy, physiology and neuroscience strengthen the argument for making movement an integral part of the learning process. In recent years there have been both clinical and educational trials demonstrating the importance of engaging both the mind and body in the learning environment.

Children who miss out

It is also becoming abundantly clear that where children have missed out on movement experiences, learning difficulties can follow. When children have opportunities to engage in spontaneous, free flow movement play, neurological development is prompted. The movement patterns they engage in are innate and naturally occurring, but for some children these opportunities are not nearly as abundant as they should be for healthy development.

Young children need to move while lying on their backs and tummies. They need to crawl, spin, tilt, lose their balance and get dizzy. They need to push, pull and stretch. Early movement play stimulates the step by step development of the nervous system and prepares the brain for future functioning. Take, for instance, children who do not crawl – the little bottom-shufflers that one day, just get up and walk! When this happens, difficulties can sometimes ensue. Crawling supports development in a variety of ways; for example, it is essential to eye-teaming development for reading and writing.

Brain Gym

Over recent years there has been a great deal of interest in Brain Gym, a therapeutic, re-patterning programme originally designed to help children experiencing learning difficulties. Paul Dennison developed Brain Gym in the 1970s when he was working through his own problems with dyslexia and other visual difficulties, and since then his techniques have helped children and adults alike. When learners have difficulty assimilating and integrating new information into the neural network, his simple physical exercises can sometimes show powerful

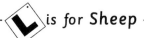
is for **Sheep**

results. Movement-based learning is not a panacea to solve all learning difficulties, but it is a potent tool at our disposal. The moment we acknowledge the powerful relationship between brain and body and begin to integrate movement into our programmes we enhance our effectiveness as educators! With a little imagination movement can be used to support any area of learning, phonics included. The activities in this chapter will give you some starting points from which to develop your own ideas.

The importance of steady beat

We all need a sense of steady beat when performing any task involving sophisticated movement; for example, walking, dancing, writing, cutting with scissors or hammering in a nail. In fact, it is so essential that if someone lacks beat competency (the ability to maintain a steady beat) he or she will usually have difficulty with both gross and fine motor skills.

Research from High/Scope in the USA suggests that a young child's ability to keep a beat is a powerful indicator for later academic success, which will come as no surprise to most early year's practitioners. It is generally more than apparent that children who are able to keep time often have a maturity and language competence beyond that of their peers. However, the exciting news is that this is a factor we can influence. By implementing a well thought-out programme of appropriate activities we can help all children to improve their beat competency, and in doing so enhance their learning.

Steady beat and language development

Steady beat underpins our ability to pick up the patterns of sound in language. This is really important, because if children cannot do this they will experience difficulty when it comes to reading and writing. English is a collection of sounds from lots of different languages, and despite the simplicity of its grammar the irregular relationships between its graphemes and phonemes make it a very challenging language to learn to read and write. This makes it even more important for us to ground English on a steady beat. One of the key stages of phonological awareness is the ability to discriminate syllables – the 'beats' within words.

A sense of rhythm

An appreciation of rhythm also helps children to recognize rhyming patterns, and this is critical to the learning of phonics. Therefore, in the light of what we know about the importance of beat and rhythm, we should provide children with a host of activities designed to develop both. Every early years setting includes movement and action songs in its programme, but once you realise how much these activities support the development of phonological and phonemic awareness, you will do them all the more. Move, dance, march and rap - and notice the difference!

The activities which follow appear in developmental order to help practitioners to match them to the needs of their children. As you try them out, remember that it is important to be consistent. You will need to do them 'little and often' for maximum effect, and having **fun** should be paramount. If the children are not enjoying themselves – **stop!** It is worth keeping in mind Marion Dowling's wise words:

> *The precious inclination to learn dissipates quickly when a child is bored or befuddled. Adults need to develop a 'red alert' to the signs of either.*

L is for **Sheep**

3 simple movement games for helping children with sound discrimination

Dodgems

What you need: A tambourine, drum or bell.

What you do: Explain to the children that when you bang the drum, or similar instrument, they are able to move around the room pretending to be dodgem cars.

Stress the importance of not bumping into each other. Make the sound again to signal **STOP**. Repeat, giving recognition to children who respond to the signal immediately.

Traffic Lights

What you need: No special resources.

What you do: Explain to the children that they are going to be cars driving along the road, but they must remember to respond to the traffic lights. Go on to explain that when you shout '**red**' they must stop straight away and freeze. When you shout '**amber**' they are to bend down and touch the floor and when you shout '**green**' they can start to move again.

Farmyard

What you need: A set of picture cards of different animals.

What you do: Explain to the children that you are going to give them a picture of an animal and that they are going to look at it and pass it back to you without telling anyone what was on their card.

On a signal from you they stand up and make the noise of their animal.

Explain that the object of the exercise is to get into a group with all the other children making the same noise as they are.

Once the children have developed phonemic awareness this can be played with phonemes.

Promoting phonological awareness through movement, beat and rhyme

Action Raps and songs are a brilliant way to promote both phonological awareness and steady beat. When children learn rhymes in conjunction with movement the multi-sensory nature of the exercises makes it much more memorable. As Colin Rose says,

'If we want to create strong memory we should store the information using all the senses. When you have heard it, said it, seen it and done it - you've got it.'

Here are some action raps for you to try with the children. In the first instance, let them perform the actions as they perform the rhyme. Once you have done this a few times the children will soon be chanting the rhymes for themselves.

Rap 1
Hands at the front
Hands at the back
Hands at the front
Then clap, clap, clap
Hands up high
Hands down low
Then wind the bobbin round
Let's go, go, go!
(Repeat)

Rap 2
Put your hands on your hips
Sway from side to side
Get on your pony
And ride, ride, ride
Hold on tight
Down the street
Stamp, stamp, stamp, stamp
Stamp your feet.

Rap 3
Wobble like a jelly
Swim like a fish
Turn right round
Blow a kiss
Pull on a rope
Arms in the air
Clap your hands
Comb your hair.

Rap 4
Spin like a helicopter
Going round and round
Then bend right down
And touch the ground
Now back up again
And run on the spot
And keep on going
Till you hear me
Shout... STOP!

Some beanbag raps

Children need a beanbag each

Beanbag Rap 1
Put your beanbag up high
Put your beanbag down low
Put your beanbag up high
Put your beanbag down low
Front and back
High and low
Front and back
High and low
Front and back
High and low
Now lift it up
And let it go!

Beanbag Rap 2
Round your head
Under your leg
Touch your nose
Then your toes
Round your head
Under your leg
Nose and toes
That's how it goes.
(Repeat as many times as you like)

Beanbag Rap 3
Make a circle with your beanbag
Move it round and round
Now bend right down
And touch the ground
Stamp on your beanbag
One, two, three
Then pick it up
And tap it on your knee
One, two, three
One, two, three
One, two, three
Tap it on your knee!

Beanbag Rap 4
Throw your beanbag
High in the air
Watch it land
Leave it there
Creep right up to it
Hold it in your hand
Now go and put it down
Where you'd like to stand
(Children then repeat the rap from their new space)

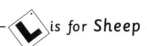

Four raps which are more challenging, using plastic plates and sticks

Rap 1

What you need: a plastic plate each.

Tap your plate
With your toe
Pick it up (*children pick up their plates*)
Don't let go
Hold it near
Hold it far
Turn the key (*children pretend
to switch on the ignition*)
Drive your car.

Rap 2

What you need: a plastic plate
and one small stick each.

Tap your plate
With your stick
Tap it, tap it
Hear it click.
Tap your plate
Tap it low
Tap your knee
Tap your toe.

Rap 3

What you need: two sticks each.

Tap your sticks together as you listen to the beat
Now tap your knees and tap your feet
Tap your sticks together as you listen to the beat
Now tap your knees and tap your feet
Tap knees, tap feet, tap knees, tap feet
Tap knees, tap feet, tap knees, tap feet
Tap your sticks together and keep it neat
Tap your sticks together and feel that beat.

Rap 4 (to the rhythm of 'Wind the Bobbin Up')

What you need: two sticks each.

Wind your sticks around
Wind your sticks around
Tap, tap
Stamp, stamp, stamp.
Wind them back again
Wind them back again
Tap, tap
Stamp, stamp, stamp.

Point to the sky
Point to the floor
Wind your sticks around
Just one more
Wind them back again
Turn around
Put your sticks down
On the ground.

Moving with Fabric

What you need: Scarves, net curtain, off-cuts of 'floaty' material. A recording of different types of music e.g: fast and slow music, jazz, classical, disco, latin, choral.

What you do: Let the children explore the different types of fabric and choose the one they would like to move with.

Explain that they will hear lots of different types of music and that they can move their fabric to the music in any way that they would like to. Once they have experienced this, encourage them to think about and talk about the ways in which the different music influenced the way they moved.

This activity will:

Help children to hear and discriminate different sounds; help develop manipulative skills and the hand-eye co-ordination necessary for later work in literacy.

Using Ribbons & Streamers

What you need: Ribbon sticks, florists' ribbon or streamers of crepe paper.

(Ribbon sticks can be made really easily! Buy some lengths of dowel from a hardware shop and cut them into 25cm lengths. Drill a hole through one end of the dowel, push the ribbon through the hole and tie in a knot). Different sorts of music.

What you do: Have the children find a space and let them explore the space around them with their ribbon stick or streamer. Once they have explored the space around themselves encourage them to move around the room exploring different levels and pathways. Work in a circle and encourage the children to generate ideas for how the group will move.

This activity will: Develop the manipulative skills essential for writing.

Using Cardboard Boxes

What you need: A collection of cardboard boxes and a selection of music.

What you do: Explain to the children that they are going to explore different ways of moving with and around the cardboard boxes. Encourage them to offer ideas for how they would like to move with the boxes. Scatter the boxes around and let the children dance around and jump over them. Open the ends of some of the boxes, tape them to the floor to make tunnels and encourage the children to go through them as they dance.

This activity will:

Help children to make connections between the right and left hemispheres of the brain and support eye-teaming.

Using Pom-poms

What you need: Some pom-poms made out of shredded material. (Cut lengths of material into strips and tie them tightly and securely in the middle. Double the material over and tie off again to make a 'handle'). Latin or carnival music.

What you do: Give each child a pom-pom. Play the music and let them explore all the different ways in which they can move with the pom-poms. Encourage them to explore at different levels and in different directions. Form a circle and lead the children in a circle dance. Model movements for them to copy. Once they have got the idea of this, let the children take turns to take the lead.

This activity will:

Develop manipulative skills; support right/left brain integration; develop a sense of rhythm and pattern essential for later work in literacy.

 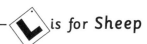

Phonemic Awareness Through Movement

Movement Instructions

What you need: No equipment

What you do: Explain to the children that you are going to give them movement instructions and that you will do it bit by bit. Go on to explain that they will need to blend the sounds together. For example r/u/n, s/k/i/p, h/o/p, etc.

Animal Movements

What you need: Picture cards of animals. Suitable music.

What you do: Explain to the children that they can move freely to the music and that they have to freeze when the music stops. Once everyone has stopped, pick a card and see if the children can move like that animal. Once the children are used to the game replace the picture cards with initial sounds. Precede as before, this time seeing if the children can think of an animal beginning with that sound and then move like that animal.

Beanbag Balance

What you need: A beanbag for each child and some quiet, gentle music.

What you do: Explain to the children that they are going to move to the music as they balance their beanbag on different parts of their body.

Ask for suggestions for all the different places where they could balance their beanbag - head, shoulder, the back of the hand, foot, nose, ear, etc.

Shout out a body part and start the music. Allow enough time for the children to explore what it feels like to balance the beanbag on that part of their body, and then swap to a different body part.

Once the children are familiar with this game, shout out an initial sound. For example: put your beanbag on a part of your body beginning with 'f.'

This activity will:
Develop manipulative skills; support the development of phonemic awareness.

Movement Sentences

What you need: A series of cards with movement words written on them - twist, roll, jump, wriggle, rock, walk, shake, bounce, etc. Some blank cards. A collection of musical instruments or soundmakers.

What you do: Explain to the children that they are going to make up some 'movement sentences' by choosing cards and joining a series of movements together.

Read out the words that are already written on the cards and invite the children to think of further movement words that can be written on the blank cards.

Invite one of the children to pick a card and have everyone move in the way it says on the cards.

Continue to pick cards, joining each movement together as you go. Once the children are familiar with the game, replace the words with initial sounds and see if children can think of movements beginning with that sound. Link the movements together.

More Phonemic Awareness Through Movement

Human Phonemes

What you need: Phoneme cards.

What you do: Put the children into pairs or small groups and give each group a card with a phoneme written on it. See if they the group can use their bodies on the floor to make their phoneme. Get them to join sounds together to make 'human words'! Use a digital camera to record their letters and words.

Finger Play

What you need: Some flash cards with movement words written on them - pointing, patting, cutting, winding, tapping, snapping, tickling, pinching, squeezing, tracing, stroking, scratching, pulling, poking etc.

What you do: Have everyone find their own space on the floor and explain to the children that they are going to concentrate on movements that can be made with their fingers.

As the music is played you will draw cards from the box and shout out the word so that they can make that movement. As each new card is drawn the children change their movement.

Once the children are familiar with the activity use only initial or final sounds and see if they can think of movements beginning with these sounds.

Fun with Newspaper

What you need: Newspaper and sellotape. Phoneme cards.

What you do: Put the children into pairs or small groups and give each group a phoneme card. See if they can make their phoneme from rolled up newspaper. Support them to put phonemes together to make simple CVC words.

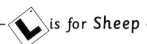

How Many Words Can We Make?

What you need: Large phoneme cards, laminated, punched and with ribbons, so that the children can wear them. Some lively music.

What you do: Explain to the children that they can move freely while the music plays but they must 'freeze' when it stops. Look for a child wearing a consonant and tap them on the shoulder. That child then looks for a vowel and taps them on the shoulder. The two then identify a third child who can join them to make a word.

Continue to pick cards, joining each movement together as you go.

Once the children are familiar with the game, replace the words with initial sounds and see if children can think of movements beginning with that sound. Link the movements together.

L is for Sheep

Kym Scott & Judith Stevens
Stages, not ages

Kym Scott and Judith Stevens are Early Years Advisers providing training and support for schools and the non-maintained sector in South East London. Their varied careers in childcare total more than forty years, and cover work as a child-minder, nanny, pre-school assistant, nursery and reception teacher and literacy adviser.

Judith writes extensively for early years publications, and in addition to a shared interest in early reading has a passion for developing mathematics outdoors. Recently Kym's interest has focussed on the development of continuity and progression through the Foundation Stage and into Key Stage 1. She contributes to national conferences as a keynote speaker and workshop leader.

Judith and Kym are co-authors of *A Place to Learn: developing a stimulating learning environment* and *Focus on Planning: effective planning and assessment in the Foundation Stage* (both Lewisham LEA, 2002 and 2004).

Kym and Judith begin by examining and describing the factors that inhibit learning. They then go on to reveiw the stages through which a child passes on the way to developing phonological awareness. They look at the importance of the balance between child initiated and adult initiated learning, and identify key experiences to support children in exploring and developing phonological awareness independently. They conclude with ideas for activities to put these theories into practice in ways appropriate to very young children, and suggest some useful resources.

Young children do not learn by being told, they learn by doing. They are active learners, who use all their senses to help them understand the world around them. They need first hand experiences, both indoors and outdoors, through which they can explore, investigate, discuss, predict and make decisions. Props and objects help to focus children's attention, engage them emotionally, make experiences more interesting, and generate enthusiasm by making learning more fun.

Brain research carried out over recent years highlights the fact that learning happens when connections (neural pathways) are made between brain cells. Continuous positive experiences exercise and firm up those connections until they are strong and permanent. Therefore, children's learning is likely to be of a higher quality in an environment which is exciting and engaging, with adults who are interested and interesting. Conversely – and not very surprisingly – research has also shown that being put under pressure has a negative impact on the development of these brain connections.

Stressful situations for young children might include:

- Having to sit still and quietly for long periods of time
- Being unable to be very active
- Not being able to make decisions for themselves
- Having to be involved in a task which does not interest or motivate them
- Being unable to succeed at tasks
- Finding it difficult to concentrate
- Not being able to understand or relate concepts to their own experiences.

For these reasons, the activities suggested in this chapter are generally intended to be used with small groups of children, although some are also appropriate for use with larger groups or individuals. As it is very unusual for any of the activities to meet the needs of all the children, whole class/large group teaching is not generally suitable. Children should not be expected to concentrate for long periods, particularly when the activities are less physical. Sessions work best when they are short and frequent, to keep children interested and motivated. Practitioners should pick up and respond to children's signals and finish activities before they become restless.

Stages not ages

In order for phonics teaching to be effective, children need to have experience of playing with sounds in each of the different stages of phonological awareness, so that they are learning to distinguish between smaller and smaller units of sound.

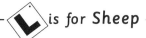

These stages are:
- Developing auditory awareness (general sound and speech sound discrimination)
- Developing awareness of rhythm and beat (syllabic awareness)
- Developing rhyming skills (awareness of onset and rime)
- Developing phonemic awareness (awareness of alliteration and individual phonemes).

All the experiences suggested later are appropriate to children at different developmental stages throughout the foundation stage, and will also support some children in Year One. There are four sections, but these are not intended to be worked through in an exact chronological order. Children learn in different ways, at different times, and the experiences within each section complement and support others.

For example, for many children new to nursery, it is appropriate to be planning to develop general auditory awareness and listening skills. But this should not be done in isolation - the same children will also needs lots of opportunities to engage in and explore rhythm and rhyme through songs, rhymes, games and rhyming and rhythmic books. In the same way, later on in Reception classes children need experience of more rhythm and rhyme as well as opportunities to develop phonemic awareness.

Most activities are generally appropriate for either children in nursery or reception, but practitioners should plan to start where the child is. If children have not developed their listening skills sufficiently by Year One, for example, it is important to offer lots of opportunities to develop general auditory awareness. This is particularly important when planning for children in Reception or Year One who are not 'clicking' with working with individual phonemes. Often they are given more of the same, when really they need to have more opportunities to work at earlier stages, developing confidence with general rhythm and rhyme before hearing smaller units of sound.

Child initiated learning

Many of the experiences suggested in this chapter outline adult initiated experiences. The aim is to make them interesting so that children want to revisit and develop them.

The government funded EPPE research (DfES: 2003) identified that practitioners in the most effective early years settings ensure a balance between adult initiated and child initiated activities. Additionally, the study emphasised the importance of practitioners supporting and extending child initiated experiences:

Freely chosen play activities often provided the best opportunities for adults to extend children's thinking. Adults need, therefore, to create opportunities to extend child initiated play as well as teacher initiated group work, as both have been found to be important vehicles for promoting learning.

Therefore, when planning to develop children's phonological skills through the suggested activities, practitioners should also ensure that children have opportunities to revisit the experiences independently.

In addition, the following experiences should be available to support children in exploring and developing phonological awareness independently:

- High quality rhyming and rhythmic texts should always be available (see the lists on page 153)

- Tapes and CDs of these stories, as well as nursery rhymes and songs, should be available in the listening area, and copies of these (with the words) should be available for families to use with children at home

- Posters of nursery rhymes and popular songs should be displayed at child level

- Story props to support core rhyming books and rhymes should be available in the book area

- Interactive displays could focus on one particular rhyme or book e.g. *Incey Wincey Spider* could be supported by a laminated copy of the rhyme, an information text about spiders, a length of plastic drain pipes, a plastic spider or hand puppet, a shallow tray, an umbrella, and a watering can

- Children should have opportunities to explore rhythm through a music area indoors and large scale music outdoors. This could include resources such as metal and plastic bins and beaters

- An indoor and outdoor 'Performance Area' with stage blocks and plastic microphones will encourage children to revisit favourite rhymes and songs

Outdoors

The outdoor environment provides meaningful and engaging experiences for young children. Many children not only prefer to spend time outdoors, but actually function at their highest level and learn best when they are outside. Of course, any of the experiences and games suggested can be repeated outdoors as well as inside. But the joy of outdoor play is that experiences can complement and extend indoor play. Children can explore on a larger, noisier, messier and generally grander scale than indoors. Practitioners should capitalise on this when planning for outdoor learning. For example, children can often hear syllables far more easily if they are shouting names rather than speaking quietly. All activities to support

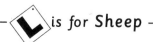

rhythm can be louder without disturbing others – children can explore rhythm by crashing saucepan lids or beating metal dustbins with wooden beaters. Favourite rhymes and books can be recalled with very physical activities – 'frogs' jumping from real logs or intrepid explorers going 'on a bear hunt' all around the outdoor area.

Resources

All of the experiences and games in this chapter use objects and props. Many of them are similar, and should be stored in clearly marked containers so that they can be easily found by both adults and children.

Children need opportunities to develop a shared vocabulary, so practitioners should aim to collect and use familiar objects wherever possible.

It is important to include soft toys, puppets, props, photos, natural items and 'real' objects and to present these attractively using wooden bowls and wicker baskets as well as plastic containers.

Responding to Sound

Before they can be expected to hear the individual word and sounds within the word children must learn to differentiate the sounds they hear around them, and respond to the stream of words in ordinary speech, . All children will pass through a similar pattern of development, but at different ages.

Adults need to plan systematically to support children's development of listening skills and their ability to distinguish between general and speech sounds. Much of this work will link in with the early learning goals for communication as well as those for linking sounds and letters.

These experiences will be useful. There are lots of possible extensions for each activity.

Developing Auditory Awareness

(sound and speech-sound discrimination)

Old MacDonald Had a Farm

Sing the song, encouraging children to join in with the sounds of the animals. Give selected children soft toys, plastic animals or puppets representing farm animals.

Choose an animal sound for the next verse, let the children identify it, before singing that verse. Encourage the children holding the toys to hold them up as the animals are identified.

Ask a child to make the next animal sound and the others identify it before singing the next verse.

What Made that Sound?

You need a small collection of sound making objects - keys, bell, squeaky toy, clock.

Spend some time familiarising the children with the names of the objects and the sounds that they make. Ensure that all the children are using the same vocabulary.

Now make the sound unobserved, the children guess the object.

What's Behind the Curtain?

Have two sets of identical instruments, one each side of the curtain.

Before starting, make sure the children can identify the sound each instrument makes. Play one instrument behind the curtain, choose a child to repeat the sound.

Now play each instrument, laying them down in sequence, and ask a child to repeat all four/five. Raise the curtain to check!

Where is the Clock?

The children close their eyes.

The adult sets a timer and hides it. When it rings, the children point to where they think the timer is hidden.

Where is the Sound?

The children sit in a circle.

One child sits in the middle and covers their eyes. The adult gives one child in the circle a sound making object such as a tambourine.

The child makes the noise, very quietly, getting louder. The child in the centre points to the sound. The children swap places.

is for Sheep

What's Behind the Curtain? (2)

Place a cloth or screen in front of the children & make a range of everyday sounds for them to identify e.g. water pouring or tearing paper.

Who do you see?

(based on the book 'Brown Bear, Brown Bear' by Bill Martin Jr.)

Children sit in a circle. The adult holds a bear puppet or soft toy and looks at one child (e.g. Charlie)

'Charlie, Charlie, who do you see?'
Charlie replies, 'I see Keisha looking at me.'
The adult passes the bear to Charlie.
Charlie chooses another child, and repeats the chant.

Snap!

Put six instruments on a tray. Familiarise the children with all the sounds and instrument names. Children close their eyes. The adult makes three sounds in a row. One child tries to repeat the three sounds. If they are correct, all shout 'Snap!'
Continue until the correct sequence is complete.

Remember that any game with simple sound makers or instruments will help with auditory discrimination.

Spot the Mistake

Give every child a small beanbag to hold. Explain that you are going to read a story, but you are a bit tired and might make some mistakes! The children will need to listen really carefully, so they can help if this happens, putting the bean bag on their head (or balancing on their nose, tossing it in the air etc) if you say the wrong thing.
Read a very familiar story, making the occasional mistake - e.g. The Three Billy Goats Bluff.
Who notices? What should you have said instead?

If I Say Your Name

Try out a sequence of activities using a bean bag with a small group of children. For example, throw it in the air, balance it on your head, pass it under one leg.
Now give 'instructions' such as:
'In the air ... Cheri.' (Always give instructions first, to ensure all children are listening.)
Then repeat, 'In the air ... everyone.'
Vary the speed, tone and volume of the instructions.

Shaker Pairs

Gather a variety of fillings - e.g. rice, pebbles, large wooden beads, pasta. Collect a set of identical containers, ideally short Pringle tubes (or yoghurt pots, film containers, etc.) and paper to cover the pots or stickers to label them.
Children choose a partner and select one filling for both of their containers. Each child makes a shaker. (Spend some time discussing the different sounds the shakers make.)
Make sure there is a pair of each type of shaker, which have the same fillings.
The adult shakes one shaker, then selects a child to hunt out the matching shaker by shaking them all.

Sounds Trail

Put a selection of objects to represent sounds in a wicker basket. Take a group of children for a walk around your setting, stopping at intervals and listening for specific sounds. When a child identifies a sound, they search in the basket for an item to identify it.
Everyone discusses whether the object is appropriate.

Sound Environment Lotto

Children take photographs outside. The adult makes a sound tape with the children, and edits as necessary at a later date. Each lotto board has six photographs of things that make sounds in the children's local environment.
Children place a counter on the picture of the sound as it is played and identified.

Nanopops

Introduce a puppet or soft toy of a strange creature or monster. Tell the children about these imaginary monsters called Nanopops, who make very strange noises.
Children invent, memorise and copy some vocal sounds.
Children sit in a circle and pass around a plastic microphone, while they chant this:
'Nanopops sing, nanopops shout,
We all sing when the rhyme runs out -
In, out, in, out, in, out, SHOUT!'
When the chant stops, the child with the microphone makes a noise to be copied.

Sam: Brrrrrrrrrr...
All: Brrrrrrrrrr...

The microphone continues round the circle and the children chant again.

Honey Pot Game

Children sit in a circle.
One child sits in the centre with their eyes shut, and plastic jar with a label saying 'Honey' on it (or bean bag) in front of them.
Children chant:
'Isn't it funny how a bear likes honey?
Buzz, buzz, buzz, I wonder why s/he does. Go to sleep Mr/s Bear, go to sleep...'
An adult walks around the circle, and quietly taps one child on the shoulder. The child creeps up to the jar/bean bag, grabs it and runs round the circle to return to their original place.
Children chant:
'Wake up Mr/s Bear, your honey's not there!'
The 'bear' chases the child back to their place. The second child becomes the 'bear'.

Fruit Salad

Children are in a circle. Pairs of real objects - e.g. 2 bananas, 2 oranges, 2 apples, etc. are distributed to the children.
An adult (or child) calls out the name of one of the fruit. Children with that fruit swap places. The caller chooses two fruits and four children swap.
When the caller calls 'fruit salad' all the children swap.

Rumble in the Jungle

As for the 'Fruit Salad' game, but children have an animal - an elephant, tiger, lion, giraffe, etc.
Adult (or child) calls out one or two animals at a time.
When adult calls 'Rumble in the jungle', all children with animals swap places.

Sound Effects Story

Choose a story with some repeated sound effects.
Choose a few sound effects for key words or actions in the story.
Have real items, or instruments to represent characters or actions in the story.
Give children the role of sound effect artistes.
For example, in the Billy Goats Gruff, a tambourine for the words 'up jumped the troll' and two half coconuts for 'trip trip' over the bridge.
Let the children take the lead sometimes.

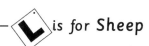

Developing Awareness of Rhythm and Beat

(leading to syllabic awareness)

A Sense of Rhythm

One of the core ways of developing children's general sense of rhythm will be through the provision of a wide range of musical experiences, the importance of which cannot be over emphasised.

Adults should also plan to develop children's phonological awareness at the syllabic level. This will help children to develop the ability to separate words into units or 'beats'. This skill is fundamental for literacy development and needs to be worked on specifically.

By helping children to learn to blend and segment larger chunks of sound, such as syllables, practitioners are helping them to develop the skills necessary to blend and segment individual phonemes (sounds) later on.

Robot Speak
Say words such as children's names or animal names slowly, breaking into syllables e.g. Sa-man-tha.
Use a toy robot as a prop to help engage the children in this. Children need to blend the syllables together to make the word. This is helpful in developing children's ability to blend sounds together to make a word later, when they will be working with much smaller units of sound.

Using Raps
Sing well known nursery rhymes as raps (e.g. Humpty Dumpty on Keeping the Beat CD). Have a soft toy or puppet to encourage children to join in.
Introduce a range of raps to children (try Ros Bayley's Animal Raps).

Beat Baby
Choose a toy or puppet to use to engage children visually and emotionally whenever you are working on beat competency skills (see Ros Bayley's Beat Baby).
Sit the children in a circle, and bring the toy out to the same rhythmic chant each time. Pass the toy around to the beat of a rhythmic chant.

Bucket Drums
Collect five or six saucepans, plastic buckets, washing up bowls, and a pair of beaters or wooden spoons for each. Choose a child for each pan/bucket/ bowl.
Encourage the children to experiment with these. Then begin to introduce a simple sound sequence e.g. pan/floor/pan/floor, etc. Say the words as they play the instruments.

Pass the Rhythm
Children sit in a circle with the adult starting a simple rhythm on a drum or a tambourine:
Tap, tap, taptap,
tap, tap, taptap...
The children clap the rhythm back. The adult passes the instrument to the next child in the circle. Everyone copies the rhythm played.

Name Beats
Children sit in a circle and pass a toy around and sing or chant:
'Let's play a game,
Tell me your name.
You clap it first,
Then we will too'.
When the chant finishes, the child holding the toy claps their name e.g. Jess-i-ca.
The group responds: **'Your name is Jess-i-ca'**
(Clapping the beats of the name)

Shaker Rhymes

Develop a set of core rhymes *(see the suggestions at the end of this chapter).* Clap these familiar rhymes with the children.

Clap the rhyme by syllables for children to guess, then clap the rhyme together and sing along.

Next clap a line at a time, children repeat.

Finally, clap one line, the children clap the next line, and so on in turn.

Keep the Beat

Use every opportunity to clap, stamp, slap thighs etc with songs, rhymes and in stories.

Clap as you walk to the hall or just around your setting.

Play clapping games with names - clap names for registration, or to choose children for an activity.

Use clapping and stamping games in your garden or outdoor area, or on walks. Clap the names of insects, birds, flowers, vehicles, shops.

Stamp patterns in puddles, in snow or frost.

Clap out weather words, sounds you hear.

Let's go on a Picnic

As above, but with picnic items (real and/or pretend) and three labelled baskets.

Items could include:

Roll, cake, cheese, grapes, coke, egg

Sandwich, biscuit, quavers, sausage, apple, orange, pizza

Banana, coconut, macaroon, pineapple, tomato, cucumber

Guess the Animal

Collect some small world animals e.g. bear, lion, crocodile.

Name the animals, ensuring shared vocabulary with the children.

Use a beater to tap out the name of each animal, one at a time. Children clap the rhythms back until they are familiar with them. Support children as they make links - e.g. **'Does anyone's name have one beat like the bear?'** Clap to check.

Provide trays labelled with '1', '2' and '3'.

Tap out the beat of one animal.

Children have to guess which animal it could be and put the animal on the correct tray.

Breakfast

Children sit in a circle, with a selection of empty mini cereal boxes in the middle. Introduce as in Guess the Animals (above), with children naming the cereals, and clapping out the beats.

Model **'I had a lovely breakfast, I had corn-flakes'**, clapping out the syllables. Then ask one child a simple question, such as **'What do you like for breakfast?'** The child claps back the beat in reply e.g. **'co-co-pops'** or **'su-gar-puffs'**.

All the children repeat their beats and guess the cereal.

Off for a Holiday

You need a selection of items for a holiday *(see list below) and* two or three suitcases/boxes, for one, two or three syllable words. Label them 1 beat, 2 beats, 3 beats.

Use a doll or teddy. Explain that s/he is packing for a holiday and wants to put all the things with one beat in their name in one suitcase and so on. Say each word and encourage children to tap the beats.

Now let the children put the items in the matching cases.

1 beat: spade, ball, hat, ring, bat, comb

2 beats: swimsuit, bucket, jumper, frisbee, armbands

3 beats: sunglasses, dungarees, umbrella, bikini.

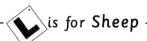 is for **Sheep**

Developing Rhyming Skills

(Awareness of onset and rime)

'Children who know lots of nursery rhymes generally read well'
Playing With Sounds DfES 2004

Research (Bradley & Bryant 1983) has found a strong predictive relationship between early rhyming and later reading. Children with good initial rhyming skills tend to become better readers and spellers. This is thought to be because these children are more easily able to make **analogies** in their reading and writing. To make an analogy in reading, a child might use the rime from a word that he knows to decode a word that he doesn't know.

For example, Sam comes across the word **'sat'** in a book. He can recognise the word **'cat'** and has a good understanding of rhyming strings, so he is able to recognise the **'at'** rime but realises that this word has a different initial phoneme. He then uses his knowledge of initial sounds to substitute the **'c'** from **'cat'** with **'s'**. Next he uses his skills of blending to put the onset and rime back together to read the word **'sat'**. Many children read new words simply by breaking them down into individual phonemes, and this should be encouraged as their main strategy. However research has shown that many children use analogies in reading spontaneously, without being taught. These children tend to have good phonological skills, particularly at the onset-rime level.

Pre-Rhyming Pairs

It is very important for children to be aware of the vocabulary involved in rhyming games. Always ensure each object is referred to by the same word. For example, if using a real object which might be referred to as a **'stone'**, children may use other words such as **'rock'** or **'pebble'** etc. Clarify the word you will all use before starting on the activitiy! For example, **rock** to rhyme with **sock**, or **stone** to rhyme with **bone**. You may also need to make allowances for regional accents and dialects, for immature speech development and for the needs of children with English as an Additional Language.

Introduce the objects as part of a feely bag game or 'surprise basket'. Ask individual children what items are called. Praise efforts: **'That's a good word, can you think of another word?'**
Ensure that all children share the chosen vocabulary.
You could also play by giving clues for children to guess the object and reinforce shared vocabulary - **'It rhymes with chair.'** etc - or play **'Kim's Game'** to reinforce vocabulary.

Rhyming Pairs

Prepare a basket and a tray, and put one of a pair of rhyming objects in each, e.g. **bell, frog and rock in the basket, and shell, dog and sock on the tray**. A child selects and names an object from the basket and finds one that rhymes with it on the tray.
Extension:
When they have done this, the children sing this song, to the tune of 'The Farmers in the Den':
Hickory Dickory Dell
Shell rhymes with bell
Bell rhymes with shell
Hickory Dickory Dell.

To play **Kim's Game** place a number of objects on a table or tray. Let the children look at them for a short time. Then cover the objects with a cloth and ask the children to remember what's there. As the children develop and get better at the game, increase the number of objects and decrease the time they have to study them – but don't try to go too far too fast.
Kim's Game develops concentration, recall and extends vocabulary.

Photo Pairs

Take photos of some objects and laminate them. First play the game very simply, with children matching real objects to individual photographs of each object:

Put the objects in the centre, spread the photos face up.

Each child selects a photo and finds the object that is the same. Extend by placing photos face down.

Once children are familiar with this concept, the game can be extended to include rhyming pairs:

Keep one half of each of the rhyming pairs of objects - the bell, frog etc.

OR Take away the other half of each pair, i.e. shell, log etc, but replace these with photos placed face down.

OR Play the pairs game as before, but this time children select a photo and find the object that rhymes with it.

Rhyming Lotto

Begin with pairs of real objects which rhyme as before.

Use photographs to make base boards and individual cards. At first, children match real objects to the same photos on their base boards.

Then move on to children selecting objects which rhyme with the photos on their base boards.

Finally, remove the objects and use photos only to play rhyming lotto.

Rhyme Robots

In your outdoor area, with a group of about eight children. Look at a collection of rhyming objects e.g. book/hook, cat/rat etc.

Discuss and name objects with children first.

Give each child an object to hold behind their back.

Explain that they are going to be robots, who need to find their partner.

Children then walk around saying the name of their object over and over again until they find the child who has the object that rhymes with theirs.

Rhyming Colours

In your outdoor area, hang large sheets of coloured card or fabric in different corners - red, blue, black, white.

Call out a word that rhymes with a colour - e.g. **bed, bread, ted, thread, queue, glue, shoe, track, mac, quack, light, kite, night, bite.** Children run to the colour that rhymes with the word.

Rhyme Fishing

Set up a water tray with blue water, shells etc. Put small objects in the water - key, stone, shell, fish, plastic number eight. Put a collection of objects which rhyme with these on a tray next to the water.

Children fish for objects using nets. When they 'catch' something they match it to the object on the tray which rhymes with it.

Odd One Out

Make collections of rhyming objects:

fox, box, socks;
frog, log, dog;
cat, hat;
bone, phone, stone;

Talk about the names of the objects. Make collections of those that rhyme. Put the items back in the basket

Use a toy or puppet. Explain that s/he is going to play a joke on them. Set up four items behind a cloth (three that rhyme, one that doesn't). Ask the children which one the puppet has put there as a joke.

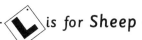 is for Sheep

I-Spy

Collect some objects - fork, car, bin, etc. Talk through the names of the objects.
Play, 'I spy with my little eye, something that rhymes with...'

Going Shopping

Gather a range of real or plastic food items and a shopping basket or wicker basket. Ask children to help a puppet or soft toy to buy some shopping.
Explain that s/he can't remember which things to get and ask the children to help find them by listening to the words and then choosing the right food.

'Smelly, welly, belly, melly,
shall we have some orange jelly?'
'Risps, tisps, wisps, frisps
Here's some cheese and onion...'
'Bapple, capple, dapple, fapple
Let us buy a crunchy...'

It is important to set up a pattern and an expectation of rhyme, and some children may need shorter rhyming phrases such as:

'Smelly, welly orange jelly....'
'Cred, Fred, A loaf of ...'

Musical Rhymes

Make sure the children are familiar with the books from the **Rhyme and Read Together Stories Series** (e.g. 'Mig the Pig') by Colin and Jacqui Hawkins.
Have a tape or CD player, and a collection of rhyming objects, if possible toy animals and an object which rhymes with each of them - e.g. a hen and a pen, a fox and a box, an owl and a towel, a dog and a log, a cat and a hat, bear and a pear.

Introduce each animal in turn, giving them a rhyming name - e.g. Pat the cat, Nog the dog.
Explain to the children that they are going to help each of the animals to find something that rhymes with their name. Have the objects which rhyme with them on a covered tray.
The children sit in a circle, and an animal is passed around the circle until the music stops. Whoever is holding the animal then uncovers the tray and finds the object which rhymes with it.
When the child has found the matching object, encourage the children to join in with a repeated refrain which reinforces the rhyme

'Mig the pig has got a wig! Did you ever see a pig in a wig?'

Microphone Rhyming Game

Put some interesting objects, (e.g. a shell, box, sock, ring, sweet etc) in an old handbag, drawstring bag or gift bag. Attach this to a toy or puppet and explain to the children that the toy has some exciting things in his/her bag and has got a great idea for a game with them. Get one object out. Can the children help to think of words which rhyme with it? Explain that to make the game even more fun she/he has brought a microphone for the children to use (use a real plastic microphone, a toy microphone, a home made one, or even a hair brush!).

As you bring each item out of the bag, the children pass the microphone around the circle, each saying a word to rhyme with the object. Less confident children may copy other's ideas until they develop their own. Encourage children to make up words if they can't think of real ones, and use this as a discussion point. When the children run out of rhyming words, bring the next object out.

Developing Phonemic Awareness

(awareness of alliteration & individual phonemes)

There may be some young children in your setting who are already interested in hearing initial letter sounds **(phonemes)** and in knowing the sounds that written letters **(graphemes)** make. This will often be linked to their own name - 'Luke is like Lydia, so is Lucozade'. Other connections are made with familiar words 'that looks like Sainsbury's (or McDonalds)'. These are often the first words children recognise and read.

Children should be encouraged to make these associations orally and aurally, as well as identifying familiar letters in meaningful situations.

Using Traditional Tongue Twisters

Share tongue twisters with children on a regular basis. Ask children what they notice about the poem. Ask why they think they are called tongue twisters. Play with the tongue twisters, saying them very quickly, very slowly, in different voices. Encourage the children to make lists of alliterative words and put these together to make a whole group tongue twister.

Here are some traditional tongue twisters:
Peter Piper picked a peck of pickled peppers.
Did Peter Piper pick a peck of pickled peppers?
If Peter Piper picked a peck of pickled peppers,
Where's the peck of pickled peppers Peter Piper picked?

Down the slippery slide they slid
Sitting slightly sideways;
Slipping swiftly see them skid
On holidays and Fridays.

Betty Botter bought some butter,
But, she said this butter's bitter;
If I put it in my batter, it will make my batter bitter,
But a bit of better butter will make my batter better.
So she bought a bit of butter,
Better than her bitter butter,
And she put it in her batter, and it made her batter better,
So 'twas better Betty Botter
Bought a bit of better butter!

Hairy Bear

Read **'Hairy Bear'** by Joy Cowley. Encourage the children to join in with phrases such as 'fim-fam-fight 'em', 'bim-bam-bash 'em' etc.
Make up other phrases - e.g. 'You know if it were me I wouldn't fim-fam-fight 'em, I would crick-crack-crash 'em!'
'Slim-slam-slom 'em'
'Mish-mash-mosh 'em' etc.
Make up your own version of the book.

Read the book **'Ketchup on Your Cornflakes'** by Nick Sharratt.
Play with other phrases, bringing in the concept of alliteration e.g. 'Do you like beetles in your bed?' 'Do you like spiders in your spaghetti?'
Encourage children to create their own phrases. Make some individual or group books based on children's own sentences.

Ketchup on Your Cornflakes

is for Sheep

Print Everywhere

Ask children and parents to collect printed material from packaging, magazines, etc.

Ask for print beginning with particular letter sounds - Smarties, Sainsbury's, Savacentre, Surf, Signal. Use this to make different games. These could include:

Lotto games

Pelmanism (pairs)

Matching games where one child picks out individual letter cards from a bag, gives the sound of each, and the other children look for print beginning with the phoneme on their card.

As above, with a child picking out objects beginning with different phonemes instead of words.

Animal Names

Make a collection of plastic animals or pictures. Put them in a bag. Take them out of the bag one at a time.

Ask the children who has the same letter sound at the beginning of their name

e.g. Cow - Carrie, Clare, Calvin

This may spark some quite complex explanations. For example, names such as Charlie and Chelsea share the same 'ch' phoneme as chimpanzee, and do not begin with the 'c' phoneme, although Chloe does. However when their names are written down, the beginning of each of them looks the same!

Alliterative Phrases

Collect and share alliterative alphabet books, such as 'Zoe and her Zebra' by Clare Beaton.

Use these as inspiration for creating your own descriptive phrases with the children - Chloe's clock; Danesh's dragon; Taewo's tiger

Always ensure children are respectful of others' names.

Personalised Alphabet Charts

Make a meaningful alphabet chart with the children, by asking them to help collect items beginning with different initial phonemes.

Take close up photos of each child holding one of the items and make into a chart.

Laminate and display at child level.

You could also make individual books with chidlren's favourite objects and words.

If you make the books in PowerPoint, the children can use them on screen or printed out as a book, a poster or a frieze.

Reading & Writing Phonemes
& words
containing these)

The following ideas are suitable for children who have already developed phonological awareness e.g. children who have a strong sense of rhythm, rhyme and alliteration. The emphasis should still be on children first hearing the sounds in words, and then learning how to write these down as letters (graphemes).

'The most effective phonics instruction teaches children to identify phonemes in spoken language first, then to understand how these are represented by letters and letter combinations (graphemes).'
Progression in Phonics DfES 1999

Making collections of objects

As with the rhyming section, it is essential that practitioners build up a wide selection of real objects beginning with different phonemes which can be used in the following games. Remember when collecting objects, it is the sound that can be heard at the beginning that is important at this stage, not necessarily the letter it begins with. For example, aeroplane does not begin with the phoneme (sound) 'a', although it is written with the letter 'a'.

These objects can be used again and again, linked to different games, such as those described below. In addition, photos can be taken of them, and these can be used for games such as initial sound bingo, pairs etc, as well as for making a more personal alphabet reference chart.

Following the children's lead

Many of the experiences in this section are specific games or activities which will require some direction and support from an adult. However it is important to initially give children plenty of time to explore these resources themselves, using them to initiate their own learning. Children will often begin to develop their own games and rules, which may provide a better 'path' than that originally planned. By observing this exploratory play, and intervening where appropriate, adults will gain a picture of children's interests and preferred ways of using the resources, which should help to inform planning for an adult focused experience.

When children have experienced these games as part of a small group focus, they should have opportunities to return to them independently, in order to consolidate and extend their previous learning.

When the children are ready to work with the resources as part of a small group focus, many of the games suggested will work best if given some kind of context.

Building a little story or role play scenario around each of the ideas and games described below will give some purpose to what children are doing. For example, the children might be going to the farmers' market to buy some new animals for their farm, or they might find a wet treasure chest which has been hauled up from the bottom of the ocean. This will engage children emotionally, and is likely to have a positive impact on their learning.

Giving a context

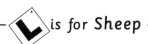 is for Sheep

Pass the Phoneme

Put a collection of objects beginning with different phonemes into a drawstring bag. Children sit in a circle, and pass the bag round to music, as in 'Pass the Parcel'. When the music stops, the child with the bag pulls out an object, establishes the initial phoneme, and passes it round the circle. Each child then thinks of another word beginning with that phoneme as they hold the object. When ideas run out, start the music again.

Confusion

Children sit in a circle and pass round a basket of pairs of objects which begin with the same phoneme, e.g. bat/bear, cat/carrot. Each child selects an object, naming it, to ensure that the child is clear of the initial phoneme. Now call out a phoneme, hold up another object beginning with the same phoneme, or an initial letter card, if appropriate. The two children with objects beginning with that phoneme swap places with each other.

Animal Phoneme Game

What you need:
Farm/zoo animals
A washing up bowl full of peat
A large builder's tray, or 4 smaller trays (e.g. cat litter trays). Natural items available from garden centres and parks such as plants; moss; cocoa shells; logs; pebbles; fir cones; rocks, etc.
Ready made initial phoneme signs; blank laminated signs, dry wipe markers.
What you do: Fill the bowl with peat and hide the animals in it. Give the tray with resources to the children and help them to set up a farmyard, with initial phoneme signs spread around. Share a story with the children about a farmer/zookeeper, whose animals are lost in the bog (bowl of peat). Can the children help to rescue the animals and put them back in the right fields? Children dip in to 'rescue' animals from the bog. Children match animals to the fields by initial phoneme.

Sorting the Laundry

Collect at least two of each of the following items of adults', children's or dolls' clothing: shirts, shorts, t-shirts, trousers, jumpers, jeans, dresses, dressing gowns, pyjamas, pants. Add these into the home corner, with washing baskets, labelled **'sh' 't' 'j' 'd'**.
Encourage children to sort the laundry into the matching basket.
You could make the Three Bears' cottage and label the baskets **'m' 'd'** and **'b'** for daddy bear, mummy bear and baby bear. Have adult, child and doll size examples of each clothing item.

Treasure Hunt!

What you need:
Box/tray for sand; sand; fish tank background from a pet shop; box for a 'treasure chest'. Items of 'treasure' beginning with different phonemes - e.g. watch, necklace, ring, money, bone, stone, feather, shell, apple and matching phoneme labels; empty film canisters or washing tablet bags.
What you do: Fill the box/tray with sand and fix the background to the tray. Hide the treasure in the sand. Roll up matching phoneme labels , put them inside the film canisters and put these in the treasure chest. Children pick a canister from the chest and 'dig' for treasure that begins with the same phoneme.

Going Shopping

Resources:
Toy or puppet, 4 shopping baskets
Food items beginning with different phonemes - e.g. apple, jelly, chocolate biscuits, beans, bread, crisps, pepper
Matching phoneme labels
Washing tablet pouches/nets (optional)   Drawstring bag
Dried pasta
Tray for food items

What you do:
Use a role play shop indoors or outdoors, or set up a table as small scale shop.
Fill the drawstring bag with dried rice/pasta. Put each phoneme label in a washing tablet pouch/net and add to the bag.
Explain how the puppet/toy wants help to go shopping.
Children 'pick a pouch from the pasta' for the puppet and buy a food item that begins with that phoneme.

Barnaby Bear's Holiday

What you do:
Prepare a teddy and a small suitcase or backpack with items beginning with different phonemes in it. Make a list of initial letters and label it 'Barnaby Bear's holiday list'. Crumpled paper adds authenticity!
Explain that Barnaby wants to make sure that he has packed something beginning with each phoneme on his list - can the children help him check?
Sit in a circle and lay the items from the suitcase on the floor in the centre.
Go through each phoneme, and ask the children to see if there is something beginning with that phoneme in Barnaby's luggage. If so, the child who finds it puts it in the suitcase and ticks that phoneme on the list.

Wrapping Presents

What you need:
Wrapping paper
Address labels
Marker pens
Sellotape
Cvc items to wrap e.g. box, fox, log, dog, cat, hat, pig, jug, mug

What you do:
Use in the role play post office or set up mini version on a table.
Children choose items to wrap up from the selection above.
Discuss how presents are usually labelled e.g. with people's names.
Children decide who each present is for and make own attempt at name label, using phonic knowledge.
Next, encourage children to write a label for the present, to say what is inside. This could be initial phoneme only, or the full word. Alternatively, adults could provide pre-written labels for children to choose from.
The presents could be put into a 'lucky dip' where other children dip in to pick out a gift, and guess who the parcel might be for and what might be in the parcel, by the label.

A Fishing Game

Fill a water tray with blue coloured water and bubbles (sea foam). Collect items beginning with different phonemes to put in the water tray. Provide plastic sieves or tea strainers as fishing nets. Label some empty baskets with different initial letters.
As you create or read a story about treasure/ships, explain that treasure is lost at the bottom of the ocean. Encourage the children to fish for the treasure and to sort it into the matching treasure baskets.

is for **Sheep**

Core Rhymes

As a team, choose a small number of familiar rhymes which are frequently used with the children. Agree your list of words and type in a big font to make A3 cards. The children can illustrate these. Use the rhymes frequently with the children, as often as a 'rhyme of the week'. Help the children to make an audio tape of the rhymes for everyone including parents and carers to use.

Collect objects and props to support the children when retelling rhymes. Use these with the children and leave them available for children to use independently.

Some possible core rhymes:

Five Little Speckled Frogs
Ten in a Bed
One Little Elephant Went out to Play
Twinkle, Twinkle, Little Star
Hickory, Dickory Dock

Five Aliens in a Flying Saucer
Five Currant Buns in a Baker's Shop
Incey Wincey Spider
Humpty Dumpty
I'm a Little Teapot

As above, work together to choose a small number of high quality rhyming and rhythmic texts (about ten or 12 titles). Add some story props and objects to support the books.

Core Rhyming Books

Possible rhyming and rhythmic texts include:

Brown Bear, Brown Bear by Bill Martin (Puffin 1992)
So Much! By Trish Cooke (Walker 1996)
Where's my Teddy? By Jez Alborough (Walker 1994)
Don't put your Finger in the Jelly Nelly by Nick Sharratt (Scholastic 1996)
This is the Bear by Sarah Hayes (Walker 1994)
We're going on a Bear Hunt by Michael Rosen (Walker 1993)
Once upon a Time by John Prater (Walker 1995)
Walking through the Jungle by Julie Lacombe
(Walker 1995)

Gruffalo by Julia Donaldson (MacMillan 1999)
Pass the Jam, Jim by Kaye Umansky (Red Fox 1993)
Bringing the Rain to Kapiti Plain by Verna Aardema (MacMillan 1986)
My Cat likes to Hide in Boxes by Eve Sutton (Puffin 1978)
Peepo by Janet and Allan Ahlberg (Viking 1983)

Other references and resources:

Puppets from Puppets by Post; www.puppetsbypost.com; Tel:01462 446040
Keeping the Beat CD from Keeping the Beat Productions; www.keepingthebeat.co.uk. Tel 0208 402 7196
Animal Raps, Action Raps, Noisy Raps and Beanbag Raps by Ros Bayley; Lawrence Educational Publications; www.educationalpublications.com - Tel:01922 643833
Helping Children with Steady Beat; Ros Bayley and Lynn Broadbent; Lawrence Educational Publications; www.educationalpublications.com, Tel:01922 643833
Progression in Phonics (DfES 1999) Tel:0845 60 222 60
Playing with Sounds: a supplement to Progression in Phonics (DfES 2004) Tel:0845 60 222 60
Mig the Pig (Rhyme & Read together Stories Series) by Colin & Jacqui Hawkins, (Dorling Kindersley 1986)
Hairy Bear - Story Chest Read Together Series by Joy Cowley (Shortland 2001)
Ketchup on Your Cornflakes by Nick Sharratt (Hippo 1996)
Zoe and Her Zebra by Clare Beaton (Barefoot Books 1999)
Bradley and Bryant (1983) in Rhyme, Rhythm and Writing (Roger Beard 1995)

L is for Sheep

Ros Bayley & Lynn Broadbent
Learning to listen with puppets

Following an extensive career as an early years teacher, Ros Bayley now works as a consultant, trainer and storyteller. She has always had a keen interest in the teaching of literacy and has written many publications for early years professionals, including *Foundations for Independence* (2nd edition 2005), *We Can Do It!* (2004), *Boys and Girls Come Out to Play* (2005) and *Smooth Transitions* (2003), all collaborations with Sally Featherstone and published by Featherstone Education. She is co-author (with Sue Palmer) of *Foundations of Literacy* (Network Continuum, 2004). Ros really enjoys writing with other professionals and has written a number of books with Lynn Broadbent (published by Lawrence Educational Publications).

Lynn Broadbent is an early years adviser with extensive experience of teaching and working with practitioners. She has co-written a number of books, which include *Flying Start With Literacy* (Network Continuum, 2005) and *Helping Young Children To Listen* (Lawrence Educational Publications, 2001). She has a keen interest in the teaching of literacy in the early years and has developed, alongside Ros Bayley, a wide variety of resources to assist professionals in this important work.

Ros and Lynn are leading experts in the use of puppets and soft toys to develop a wide range of creative, social and learning skills. In *Learing to listen with puppets* they explain why puppets are such a valuable resource and how they can be used. For thos new to this work their advice on getting started provides clear guidance and reassurance. As with all their work, the aim is effectiveness and enjoyment.

Go into any early year's setting and you will be sure to find a variety of soft and cuddly toys. There may even be a puppet or two. Now add an enthusiastic early year's practitioner – and you have a recipe for magic! Toys and puppets can captivate and inspire young children. They can be used to support just about any area of the curriculum, and tuning into sound is no exception. However, they cannot do it by themselves. In order to come to life they must be lovingly manipulated by an adult who believes in them. Once the adult has breathed life into them, they will engage the children at an emotional level and deeper learning is assured.

Using toys and puppets is both fascinating and rewarding. The children derive so much from the process that practitioners find that once they get hooked it's difficult to stop. You do not need to be a theatrical extrovert – anyone can do it. Sounds too good to be true? Well, it isn't, and what's more, it's easy! All that is needed is that you understand one or two basic principles, and once you've done this you're away. So let's get going!

Getting started

In the first instance, it's important to differentiate between those puppets that will be available for the children to play with and those that will be retained by you as a tool for promoting learning and teaching. These could be called the 'practitioner's puppets'. They should be kept in a special place and brought out for specific purposes. In this way they will retain their magic and become powerful vehicles for learning. You can involve the children in making decisions about what they should be called and where they will live. In fact, the more you involve the children the more excited they will become about your characters and your stories, and before long, they will be squealing with excitement when it's time for a session with your toy or puppet.

Choosing a character

It is really important that you choose for yourself a toy or a puppet that you feel really comfortable with. If the character does not appeal to you, you will find it difficult to be convincing and the children will not believe in it. Whether you are attracted to animal, human or fantasy characters, it is imperative that you choose a toy or a puppet that the children can relate to.

Take time to explore how easily a puppet or toy can be manipulated. In the case of a toy, try to find one that is a happy compromise between being over-stuffed and not too floppy. If it's overstuffed you will not be able to move its limbs to give it expression – if it's too floppy it will be equally difficult to manipulate! Sit it on your hand and grab it at the back of the neck between your thumb and your forefinger. This will enable you to turn its head so that it can look at the children

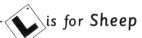
is for **Sheep**

and express itself. You can use the fingers of the hand it is sitting on to move the arms and legs. You may think that the children will be aware of you doing this, but amazingly they are always so focused on your character that they do not seem to notice at all.

If you are using a puppet, be sure to keep the body erect. If the puppet flops so that its head is sitting on its stomach it will not look realistic. Also remember to take your time – slow movements tend to be more convincing than fast jerky ones. Try locking yourself in the bathroom and practicing in front of the mirror. You'll be amazed at how good it looks! Remember, repetition is the mother of proficiency. Learning to work with toys and puppets is just like learning any other new skill. The more you practice the better you'll get.

Introducing your toy or puppet

Once you have chosen your character you will need to set it into a context, and if he or she is going to be used by more than one person it is important to involve everyone in the process. You may forget what you have said but the children will not! Answering these questions will help you to establish a credible starting point on which the children can help you to build.

- Where has the puppet come from?
- What is its background?
- What sort of personality will it have?
- What are its likes and dislikes?
- What is it good at?
- What does it find difficult?
- Does it have any family?

A home for your toy or puppet

Where will your toy or puppet live? You will need to give some thought to a suitable home. A special house, basket or box kept for this purpose will raise the status of your character. Consider also whether your character will speak and have a voice, or be silent and communicate through gesture and body expression. There is no right or wrong here, it is simply a matter of preference.

Having thought these things through you will be ready to go! Explain to the children that you have bought along a friend who is going to help them to listen and to learn about sounds. Very slowly, take your character out of the box or bag and reveal him (or her), to the children. You may feel it appropriate to pass him around so that each of the children can say hello to him. They might like to introduce themselves and tell the toy or puppet their name.

Occasionally, one of the children will say something like: 'It's not real – it's only you doing it!' Do not be thrown by this. Young children are constantly trying to make sense of the world and are exploring the difference between fantasy and reality. In response to their comments, simply answer in the way that works best for you. You may explain that you know and they know that the puppet is not real, but that you don't want to upset him by letting him know that you know! If you prefer something a little more straightforward, simply explain that you know that, but he has come to help everyone with their learning. Once you get this out of the way the children are usually more than happy to suspend their disbelief and buy into the drama!

You are now in possession of an extremely potent tool, so be prepared to be amazed. If you have never used puppets consistently before you will find that the more the children bond with your character, the more excited they will be about the work in hand. Try out some of the activities which follow and see for yourself. They are in developmental order. Simply identify the developmental level of your children and pick and choose from the menu as best meets your needs. Have fun, and remember to stop if you see the children becoming bored or befuddled. Adults need to develop a 'red alert' to the signs of either. If you and the children are not having fun, stop, and re-think the activity!

Auditory discrimination

In an increasingly noise filled world, many young children need help with basic listening skills. It is not uncommon for some children to experience difficulty with the most fundamental listening skill of all – discriminating a foreground sound from background noise. When the practitioner addresses them in a busy, bustling setting, these children may appear to ignore what is being said to them. The reality may be that they are unable to filter out the sound of the practitioner's voice and distinguish it from all the background noises. Where this happens it causes huge problems for the children concerned as they are asked to attend to a widening range of auditory information and become ever more disconnected and disorientated. The ability to make fine distinctions between sounds is essential for achieving clear articulation and phonological awareness. In helping children at this most basic level, toys and puppets can be invaluable.

Setting the scene

Start by finding a really attractive box or basket and a soft piece of material. Wrap your toy in the material and pop it into the basket or box. Sit the children in a circle, saying that there is someone you would like them to meet. Tell them that although your character is very friendly, he (or she) is also very shy. Explain that they will need to be especially quiet so as not to frighten him. Get them to pass

him around. Almost all children will be captivated by this, and you will find that it creates a quiet atmosphere for listening. It will also engage the children at an emotional level – and when the emotions are engaged – the learning is always deeper. You are now ready to introduce activities to promote some powerful learning. The ideas on the following pages will get you started.

Tuning in to Sound with Puppets and Soft Toys

Can You Hear the Bell?

What you need: A CD player, some music and a bell. (You can buy an attention bell from an office stationer's for just a few pounds).

What you do: Explain to the children that they are going to pass the toy around the circle as the music is played. They must listen very carefully for the bell and when they hear it, they must stop passing and hold the toy very still. They can begin passing again when the music resumes. Start by playing the music really softly so that the bell is easily heard - then gradually increase the volume to make the game more challenging.

Making Music

What you need: A selection of musical instruments.

What you do: Show the children a small selection of instruments. Make sure that each one makes a distinctly different sound. Place the instruments behind a screen, e.g. a piece of material draped over two chairs. Your toy then plays one of the instruments (You'll have to do it really!!) The children then guess which instrument has been played.

Who is it?

What you do: One child sits with their back to the rest of the group. As the puppet touches each child on the head they say: 'Who is it?' The child in the chair guesses the name of the speaker from the sound of their voice. They keep going until they make a mistake. The child that has been incorrectly identified then replaces them in the chair.

The Puppet & the Tape Recorder

What you need: A tape recorder and a tape recording of familiar adults reading a poem or a nursery rhyme.

What you do: Make a tape recording of familiar adults reciting a story or a rhyme. Explain to the children that your puppet has a very special tape recording he wants to play to them. Play each one to the children and see if they can identify the adults by the sound of their voices.

Change Seats

What you need: Picture cards of animals that make different sounds.

What you do: Sit on chairs in a circle and give out the picture cards. Sit your puppet on its own chair. Explain to the children that they are going to teach the puppet how to play a game. Tell them that they are going to look at their picture to see what noise their animal makes and then follow the instructions. Call out instructions for the children. For example - all those who have a picture of an animal that goes like this (moo) change seats - all those who have a picture of an animal that goes like this (woof, woof) change seats - And so on!

Quick Responses

What you need: Three different musical instruments.

What you do: The object of this game is for each of the children to perform a different movement to the sound of each of the musical instruments. Discuss how they will move to each signal, e.g. stand up quickly when you hear the tambourine, turn around when you hear the drum, jump as high as you can when you hear the recorder etc. You can do this activity without a puppet, but when the puppet plays the instruments the activity becomes much more interesting.

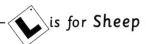
is for Sheep

Phonological Awareness

Phonological Awareness

Before children can develop phonemic awareness (the knowledge that words are made up of different sounds that can be taken apart and put together again) they must have good phonological awareness. This means that they will be aware of the sounds in language and aware of words as units of sound. They will be aware of syllables and understand that words can consist of more than one sound. They will also be aware of rhyme and will begin to play with rhyming words for themselves. (You know the sort of thing...its easy, peasy...lemon squeezy.)

Once they are doing this they are on the way to phonemic awareness and becoming aware of initial sounds. Throughout this stage they need daily opportunities for joining in with and learning rhymes and here again, puppets and toys can be invaluable.

Beat Baby

We have a small cuddly toy that we call a Beat Baby. She curls and uncurls and we use her to help develop a sense of rhyme, rhythm and beat. (For more information on Beat Babies see the resources on p153).

However, any small soft toy can be used as a Beat Baby.

What you need: A small, appealing soft and cuddly toy.

What you do: Hold the toy in your hand and recite the following rhyme.

Beat Baby, Beat Baby oh so small,

Beat Baby, Beat Baby curled up in a ball.

Beat Baby, Beat Baby can't see you at all,

Beat Baby, Beat Baby will you hear our call?

The children call Beat Baby, starting with a whisper and getting gradually louder and louder until Beat Baby uncurls herself. They then pass her around the circle to the following chant:

Beat Baby go round the circle, Beat Baby go round the circle,

Beat Baby go round the circle and say hello to us all.

Come for a Walk

What you do: Explain to the children that they are going to help the puppet learn some sounds. Decide which sounds you wish to focus on and then set off on a walk. Encourage the children to find things to show the puppet that begin with a particular sound. Take along a digital camera so they can record the objects they find for future reference/recall.

I Can't Do it!

What you do: Explain to the children that your puppet needs some help to make some rhymes. Have your puppet whisper a word in your ear and once you have shared this with the children they take turns to think of rhyming words. Get your puppet to acknowledge each child as they help him.

Traditional Tales

What you need: A selection of puppet characters for a range of puppet stories.

What you do: Tell stories using your puppets and use rhymes such as this (for the Gingerbread Man) -

> Run, run as fast as you can,
> You can't catch me,
> I'm the Gingerbread Man.

Then be adventurous and make up some of your own, for example, when telling the Three Little Pigs, the first pig might say something like:

> I have to build a house
> With nothing at all.
> I think that I could do it
> If I had some straw.
> I don't have any money
> I don't have much time
> But if you'd let me have some straw
> That house could be mine!

Once you start experimenting you can build up a good collection of raps and rhymes. However if you need some help try Ros Bayley's Almost Traditional Tales.

N.B. Once you have modelled the stories for the children, make the puppets available throughout periods of child initiated learning so that the children can retell the stories for themselves.

Alliteration with Soft Toys

What you need: A basket of assorted soft toys.

What you do: Explain to the children that they are going to think up names for the animals and that the names are going to begin with the same sound as the puppet e.g. Danny ... Dave ... Dennis Duck. Once you have thought of names for each animal see if the children can point out the letter on an alphabet frieze.

More Alliteration

What you need: The basket of soft toys.

What you do: Choose a toy from the box and explain to the children that they are going to think of words to describe the toy that begin with the same sound as the toy. For example, if the animal is a leopard you might come up with words like: lovely, lazy, little, lollopy.

Feely Bag

What you need: A bag of interesting objects beginning with different initial sounds.

What you do: As with the 'More Alliteration', explain to the children that they are going to help the puppet. He has a bag of things but he doesn't know the letter sound that they begin with. Take things out of the bag and get the children to identify the initial sound for the puppet. Link to an alphabet frieze.

The Puppet's Collection

What you need: A variety of objects beginning with the same initial/final phoneme plus some objects that don't 'fit.'

What you do: Explain to the children that the puppet likes to collect things and that he has made a collection and hidden the things he has collected all over the place and forgotten where he has put them. Prior to this you will need to hide the collection of items around the room or the outside area. Show the children photographs or pictures of the things he has collected. Alternatively make a list on a whiteboard and ask them what they notice about the collection. For example, that most things begin with 's' or 't'. Have a grand search and as each item is found it can be checked off against the list. The children can then collect additional items for the puppet's collection.

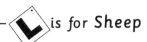

Puppet Shopping

What you need: A shopping basket or bag packed with a range of items. What you put in the bag will be determined by the initial sound that you are to focus on.

What you do: Explain to the children that the puppet has been to the supermarket and 'helped himself' to a wide variety of items that will now have to be returned. Pass the shopping around and let the children take an item out of the bag. Get the children to name the item as they take it out. Ask them what they notice about the items e.g. that they all begin with 'b' or some begin with 's' and some with 'w.' If there are a range of items see if the children can group themselves according to the item they have selected or been given. Use hoops, 'stations' or labels to assist the children with this task. If appropriate arrange the groups of things alphabetically. Make a list of all the things that the puppet has collected in the supermarket. Explain to the children that having them sorted out in this way will help the supermarket manager to know exactly what the puppet has taken out of the shop. The puppet can then thank the children for their help.

The Jumble Sale

What you need: A range of articles with CVC names, e.g. cat, dog, bus, man, pot, pen, hat, nut, peg, pin, car, tin, etc. Some labels/price tags to match the items.

What you do: Explain to the children that a friend of yours has arranged her stall for the local jumble sale and then gone for a cup of tea. While she was away your puppet had picked everything up and replaced it in the box. Distribute the items and the labels and get the children to sort them out. Ask the children what they notice about the labels, encouraging them to notice similarities and differences.

Who's Lost?

What you need: Some objects that can be labelled with CVC words e.g. toy, dog, car, cat, man, hat, pot, cup, lid, mug, tin etc.

A list that corresponds with the objects with some extra objects on the list (these are the ones your puppet has lost.)

What you do: Explain to the children that your puppet has lost some of the things from his collection but he doesn't know which ones are missing. In order to find out he needs to check the items off against the list. Get the children to read the list and check that the items are there. Then they can tell the puppet the ones that are missing.

Puppet Painted Stones

What you need: Some flat pebbles or stones with phonemes painted on them. A conch shell or something similar for the children to pass round.

What you do: The children sit in a circle and pass the 'conch' around until your puppet rings a bell or makes a similar noise. The child holding the 'conch' then selects a pebble. They could do this at random, and then the other children can think of something beginning with that phoneme, or they could choose a specific stone to make a particular word.

The above activities are simply starting points. Once you have experimented with them and you experience the power of the puppets and toys you will devise many more activities and experiences of your own!

L is for **Sheep**

Judith Harries
Sound it out

Judith Harries is an experienced teacher who has been teaching music and drama in Northampton for over 15 years. She has a particular interest in the early years and currently works with children from as young as nine months to eleven year olds.

Before she started her teaching career, Judith worked for various music publishers, including Boosey & Hawkes, Faber Music and Oxford University Press, where she was involved in commissioning and writing new products for the educational music market.

As well as teaching, Judith now edits and writes extensively for early years publications and has written several books in the *Planning for Learning* series (Step Forward Publishing), including *Role Play, Journeys, Growth, Water, Sound* and *Opposites.* She is the author of *The Little Book of Sound Ideas* (2006, Featherstone Education).

In *Sound it out* Judith offers a wide range of activities and ideas to help children develop a sense of rhythm and beat. Tapping and clapping get children making and responding to rhythmic noises. The word and listening games will encourage sensitivity to the sounds words make, while other activities focus on the sounds of letters. All these will help prepare children for reading. Finally, there is a selection of original rhymes for children to say, sing and enjoy. The emphasis throughout is on learning based on physical activity, action and fun.

In the womb, every developing baby is immersed in the strong rhythmic pulse of its mother's heartbeat. Once born, babies are rocked and soothed rhythmically, fed rhythmically, bounced rhythmically, sung to rhythmically. These are all experiences which serve to develop rhythmic awareness, and because of the supportive context in which they occur the child associates them with feelings of security.

As the child grows, singing songs and rhymes helps to develop early language skills. Through the repetition of songs and rhymes, he experiences the natural rhythms and accents of his own language. The pace is often slower than in normal speech, and this helps the learning. While trying to make sense of speech, children become sensitive to the rhythmic properties of speech and they soon begin to copy these rhythms, even if the actual sounds they are making are not correct. It is important to develop simple auditory discrimination skills at an early age. Current research suggests that children's familiarity with individual sounds and patterns of sound in speech is related to success in learning to read.

The Stepping Stones to the Early Learning Goals for Communication, Language and Literacy include several references to musical skills, such as enjoying rhythmic activities and distinguishing between sounds. Most children enjoy sound and have a natural affinity for making and responding to noises of all sorts. From very early on, young children listen to, produce and experiment with sounds. A central part of musical development is the ability to recognise the beat or pulse in music and to reproduce and create rhythm. Word rhythms are frequently used to help children improve rhythm skills as well as linguistic skills. The capacity to listen to and discern between sounds is also a key part of musical development, so that sounds can be recognised, selected, created, ordered and organised into music.

The ideas which follow aim to explore how these abilities can help develop children both creatively and linguistically. Each unit is closely linked to a Stepping Stone and includes activities and games alongside songs and rhymes. The activities vary in length from a 20 - 30 minute music session to much shorter moments that can be picked spontaneously and used when the opportunity arises. No special musical knowledge is required, and the songs are all based on tunes which will be widely familiar.

As with all the other activities in this book, the aim is for children to enjoy the learning, and through this to become competent and confident in the skills they need for learning to read.

L is for **Sheep**

Body Beats - enjoying rhyming and rhythmic activities

Body Beat Band

* Sit in a circle and ask the children to experiment with sounds using their hands such as clap, tap, rub, swish, slap, click, etc. Invite the children to take it in turns around the circle showing their sounds. Do the same with feet and other body sounds, e.g. stamp, tongue click, etc.
* Choose one or more of the sounds to make in time to the beat as you sing a well-known song or nursery rhyme.
* Ask children to copy patterns of body sounds such as 'clap, stamp, clap, tap'. Can they invent their own patterns for each other to copy? Try repeating the same patterns over and over again.
* Learn to sing and play the 'Body Beat Band'. Divide the children into two groups.

Ask one group to keep the beat with a body sound such asclap or stamp or a pattern of sounds (clap, click, clap, click). Another group can chant the words at the same time.

> **Body Beat Band**
> Listen to the Body Beat Band,
> Making sounds with feet and hands.
> Can you join us as we play?
>
> *Make a rhythmic pattern for children to copy.*

Keeping the Beat

* Listen to recorded or live music with a strong beat and encourage the children to move in response to the beat. Encourage them to experiment with free dancing or movement. Provide short ribbons attached to curtain rings or wrist bands.
* Clap or play the pulse on a drum yourself, to reinforce the feel of the beat.
* Invite the children to clap hands or tap their feet in time to the beat, or nod heads, rock or sway from side to side, whatever they feel comfortable doing.
* Can they choose an instrument to play along to the beat?
* Organise a 'keep fit' or aerobics session with the children. Select some dance music with a strong beat and ask the children to stand in a space in the room. Warm up first by shaking different parts of the body, and circling the arms gently. March up and down on the spot in time to the beat. Try two steps forwards and then backwards and to the left and to the right. And repeat. Add hoops and ribbons and have fun. You could even invite some parents to come and join you!

> **Can you Play on the Beat?**
> If you can play on the beat, beat, beat,
> It really is quite neat, neat, neat.
> And if you tap your feet, feet, feet,
> You'll play together on the beat, beat, beat.
>
> *To: A sailor went to sea, sea, sea*

> **Beat Rap**
> Bend your knees, point to the sky,
> Turn around, head up high,
> Clap your hands, stamp your feet,
> Can you do these to the beat?
>
> Click you fingers, pinch your nose,
> Scratch your head, touch your toes,
> Kick your bottom, with your feet.
> Can you do these to the beat?

Moving Beats

* Stand in a circle. Practise moving feet in time to the beat - on the spot, forwards and backwards, side to side, and around in a circle. Try the Beat-box Chant.
* Move around the circle in different ways following the leader. Start with walking or marching, then running, hopping, skipping, sliding, and dancing.

Always encourage the children to keep in time to the beat played by the drum or tambourine.

* The children sit facing a partner and sing 'Row, Row, Row the Boat'. Try and keep the rowing movement in time to a steady beat. Let a child select a different tempo and move in time to this beat. Change the words and sing 'Rock, Rock, Rock your Friend'.
* Play 'Traffic Light Sounds' using three contrasting movements and three different sounds to represent the lights.

Following the Leader

Following the leader,
the leader, the leader
We're following the leader,
whatever she may do.

Beat-box Chant

Up, down, up, down,
Turn around, turn around,
Left, right, left, right,
Day and night, day and night.
Slide, glide, slide, glide,
Side to side, side to side.
Two feet, two feet,
Keep the beat, keep the beat.

Rock, rock, rock your friend

Rock, rock, rock your friend,
Rock them to and fro.
Keep it steady, then be ready,
Now you let them go!

Copying Sounds

* Try some simple echo clapping. Clap four times and ask the children to copy you. Can they start as soon as you finish? Change the pattern and see if they can copy it. Can they copy you with their eyes shut so they have to rely on listening? Make the patterns more complicated. Try clapping and tapping knees.
* Try loud and quiet echo clapping. To create quieter sounds either use two fingers to tap or you could wear gloves.
* Play 'Echo Machines'. Make rhythmic patterns of long and short sounds using your voice for the children to copy, for instance:
  ding ding mmmmmmmmmmmmm, or ssssssss sssssssss tick tick tock.
* Play a rhythm pattern on the tambourine and invite a child to copy or echo you as accurately as they can on another tambourine. Choose different instruments to copy in pairs.
* Try echo singing. Sing two note patterns using the cuckoo notes (G falling to E or soh me) for the children to copy. Use simple hand signals: palm facing you (G - soh), hand lying flat (E - me).
* Sing echo or call and response songs, such as 'Frere Jacques' and 'I Hear Thunder'.

Echo

I hear sounds, I hear sounds,
Can you too? Can you too?
Ticka-tocka buzz buzz,
Ticka-tocka buzz buzz,
Was that you? Was that you?

To: I Hear Thunder

Can You Sing What I Sing?

Can you sing what I sing?
Can you sing what I sing?
Sing it like me! Sing it like me!
Can you sing what I sing?
Can you sing what I sing?
Sing it like me! Sing it like me!
Sing it high, sing it high,
Sing it low, sing it low,
Sing it fast, sing it fast,
Sing it slow, sing it slow,
Sing it quiet, sing it quiet,
Sing it loud, sing it loud,
Sing it shy, sing it shy,
Sing it proud, sing it proud,
Sing it happy, sing it happy,
Sing it sad, sing it sad,
Sing it good, sing it good,
Sing it bad, sing it bad.
Can you sing what I sing?
Can you sing what I sing?
Sing it like me! Sing it like me!

Children love rhymes and they are an essential part of developing phonological awareness. Here are some ideas for rhyme times:

Rhyme Zone

* Spend time each day sharing nursery rhymes, well-known songs and funny rhymes by poets such as Dr Seuss, Roald Dahl or Giles Andreae. Encourage the children to use musical instruments to accompany the rhymes.
* Make posters and displays of nursery rhymes to decorate the walls and for children to refer to when learning rhymes. Provide a 'Rhyme Rack' on a book shelf that includes books and laminated cards of rhymes for children to select and recite together.
* Tape record yourself and different voices (including children's voices) saying the rhymes for them to listen to. Let the children use a microphone and tape recorder to record themselves reciting rhymes.
* Put together Rhyme boxes including a fabric mat with the words scribed in fabric pens, a laminated card of the rhyme or illustrations, simple props, and some sound makers, and allow the children opportunity to retell, act out and perform the rhymes for each other.
* Build up a resource book of songs and rhymes to dip into. Anytime you hear, sing, or read a rhyme you could use, put a copy into your resource book or file.

Come and Sing

Come and sing a rhyme with me,
Come and sing a rhyme with me,
Come and sing a rhyme with me,
Come inside the rhyme zone.
Come and sing it on the phone,
Come and sing it, keep the tone,
Do not sing your rhyme alone!
Come inside the rhyme zone.

To: 'Bobby Shaftoe'

Listening Lab

* Set up a cosy listening area with soft chairs, cushions, soft toys and a carpet or rug on the floor. Provide tape recorder, radio and CD players so that children can listen to music. Show them how to use headphones so that they can concentrate on their listening.
* Make available a varied selection of music for the children to choose from such as classical, jazz, world, folk, and children's songs. Try to change the music on offer regularly.
* Provide children's story books and tapes or CDs for those children who prefer to listen to stories. Sit with them and share the experience. Talk about the different sounds of voices and sound effects included on the tapes.
* Make a listening game of mystery sounds for the children to listen to in the lab and try to identify. Record sounds from home such as eating cornflakes, water going down the plughole, flushing toilet, boiling kettle, door bell, etc. Add sounds from school such as children laughing, footsteps, computers, heater humming, etc. Alternatively, use a commercial sound bingo game.

Listen Well

Listen well, listen well,
Can you tell, can you tell?
Is it a phone or is it a door?
Are those footsteps on the floor?
Did he shout or did he snore?
Listen well.

To: 'Three Blind Mice'

Matching Pairs

* Collect together as many pairs of small matching containers as you can. Make matching sound pairs by filling pairs with the same amount of dry filling (e.g. lentils, beans, pasta, rice, sand, seeds, coins). Ask the children to use their ears to match the sounds.

Find my Pair

Pick me up, and shake me down,
Can you listen to my sound.
Shake and wait, make no mistake,
Can you find my pair?

To: 'Oats & Beans & Barley Grow'

Spot the Sound

* Place two or more instruments under a scarf. Play one of them for the children to identify.
* You could give each child an instrument. One child sits in the middle, wearing a blindfold. Two children play their sounds together. Can the child in the middle identify the sounds?

Hiding Sounds

Hide two sounds away,
Hide two sounds away,
Listen, listen, listen, listen,
Which one did I play?

To: Knees up Mother Brown

Two Together

Play two sounds together,
Play two sounds together,
Play two sounds together,
Then sit down.

To: Polly Put the Kettle On

Sorting Sounds

* Sit in a circle with a selection of musical instruments in the middle and take it in turns to play each instrument and listen to the different sounds it can make. Talk about shaking, scraping and tapping sounds. Sort them into groups according to how they are played and put them into hoops. Are there any instruments that can be played in all three ways?
* Choose one instrument such as the tambourine and pass it round the circle. How many different sounds can the children make from one instrument?
* Sort the instruments into groups according to the materials they are made from such as wood, metal, skin, or plastic. Invite one child to sit blindfolded in the middle of the circle. Ask one group to play their instruments. Can the listener recognise which group is playing?
* Teach some simple conducting signals such as open hands to start the sounds, and close fists to stop them. Invite the children to take turns conducting the group, choosing groups of instruments to play one at a time.

Which Sounds?

Oh, which sound shall I play today,
Play today, play today,
Oh, which sound shall I play today,
Shall I tap or shake or scrape?

Oh which sounds shall we make today,
Make today, make today,
Oh which sounds shall we make today,
Wood, metal, plastic or skin?

To: Aiken Drum

Sound Searches

* Go on a listening walk around your setting, inside and outside. Before setting off talk to the children about how to listen carefully and search for sounds by being very quiet themselves!
* Take a tape recorder and record some of the sounds you hear. Can the children recognise the sounds when you play the recording?
* Record the children's voices on tape and listen back. Can they recognise each other?

I Heard a Sound

I heard a sound as I went by,
As I went by, as I went by,
I heard a sound as I went by,
On my walk this morning.

To: I Saw Three Ships

* Challenge the children to search for sounds around your setting. Can they hear voices laughing, a child crying, someone reading a book, riding a bike, footsteps, a doorbell or telephone ringing?
* Hunt together for different types of sounds - a loud noise, a ringing sound, a rattling sound, a very quiet sound, a very high or low sound, a ticking sound, a humming sound, silence.

is for Sheep

Rhyming songs and singing rhymes help children to develop awareness of rhyme and alliteration. Try some of these:

Singing Rhymes

* Sing familiar nursery rhymes and leave out rhyming words at the end of lines replacing them with a funny sound. Can the children sing the missing words in the gap for you next time round?
* Choose two matching sounds to play instead of the rhymes each time.
* Introduce a hand puppet preferably with a moving beak or mouth called 'Noisy Nora' who sings rhymes for the children to copy and join in. Let the puppet forget rhyming words and make mistakes. The children will love correcting her.

An example of a rhyming song

Tom, Tom, the piper's <u>son</u>
Stole a pig and away did <u>run</u>
The pig was <u>eat</u>, Tom was <u>beat</u>
And Tom went howling down the <u>street</u>.

---

* Use a 'song spinner'. Make a six or eight sided spinner with divisions for boys, girls, solo, sitting down, standing up, loud, quiet, humming. Spin and sing the song following the instructions.
* Make a 'Songbag' containing song titles on laminated card, artefacts or props. Invite a child to try the lucky dip and see which song they choose. If they pull out a spider do they know which song to sing? Include a card with a ? so the child can choose one of their favourites.

Linking Letters

* Sing some rhymes which use alliteration such as Simple Simon, Jack and Jill, and Little Tommy Tucker. Ask the children to stand up every time they hear or sing a word starting with a matching letter.
* Sit in a circle and play the 'Name Game'. Set up a regular clapping pattern of two slow claps followed by two silences. Ask the children to insert their name into the gap.
* Try singing different letter sounds. Ask children to stand up tall, feet slightly apart, heads high and breathe in through their noses and out through mouths. Continue this until all children are really concentrating on their breathing. Ask them to try and hold their breath while you count to 3 or 5. Then let the air escape through an 'oh' shaped mouth. Repeat using other long sounds such as 'aaah', 'eee', 'ow', 'ssss', 'grr' and 'zzzz'.

My Name

My name starts with 'b',
Can you find another?
Boat, big, book, bee.
That was no bother.
My name starts with 'f',
Can you find another?
Fish, fat, full, farm.
That was no bother.

To: One Man Went to Mow

Rhyming Words

* Sing some well-known songs and rhymes and ask the children to stand up or make a funny action every time they sing or hear a rhyming word.
* Collect musical rhyming words such as ding, sing; crash, bash; clap, tap; pop, stop; boom, zoom; click, tick, etc. Create a pattern using your rhyming pairs. Add some instruments.

My Sound

Match my sound,
Match my sound,
Listen very carefully,
Match my sound.

To: Hot Cross Buns

Make a Sound

Rum tum tum, on the driving drum
Ring ding ding, on the beautiful bells
Tick click click, on the wild woodblock
Dangle jangle, on the tiny triangle
Rattle prattle, on the merry maracas
Tap snap snap, on the clicking claves
Have a fine time, make a good sound,
Playing in the big beat band.

Ideas for recognising rhythm in spoken words. Music helps children with rhythm, and this helps hearing, beat and readiness for reading.

Long and Short

* Rhythm is made up of long and short sounds. You can explore the difference with a triangle. Play a long note by tapping a suspended triangle and then contrast it with a short note by holding one of the sides of the triangle as you play.
* Explore playing long and short sounds on other instruments such as drums, Indian bells, cymbals or chime bars. Is it possible to play long sounds on some instruments such as claves, woodblocks and castanets?
* Ask the children to stand up and open their arms wide when the sound is long and close their hands together when the sound is short.
* Use well-known phrases to create patterns of long and short notes such as 'All aboard!' (long, short, long) 'Cock-a-doodle-doo' (long, short, long, short, long), or 'Then I'll huff, and I'll puff, and I'll blow the house down! (short short long, short short long, short short long short short short).

> **Some of These Sounds**
> Some of these sounds are short
> Some of these sounds are long
> Some of these sounds go on and on
> Can you sing this song?
> *To: Here we go Looby Loo*

More ideas for rhythm

> **Rhythm Song**
> Take a drum, make it talk,
> If you can say it, you can play it
> Take a drum, make it talk
> Listen to the talking drum.
> *To: Sur le Pont, D'Avignon*

Rhythm Talk

* Demonstrate how to clap, rattle, tap or drum the rhythm of some simple phrases such as 'Time for rest', Do your coat up', 'It's snack time!' and 'Would you like an apple?'
* Choose two or three different phrases and say and play the rhythm over and over again. Can the children tell which message you are playing without the words to help? Try giving instructions by clapping without words.
* Chant or say nursery rhymes emphasising the rhythm/beat of the words. Clap, tap, or stamp on the beat. Play the beat on instruments.
* Play 'Talking drums'. Tap children's names for registration, for snack, for grouping. To start with, look at the child whose name you are saying, then see if they can get it with a clue - eg 'I'm thinking of a girl whose name sounds like *tap/tap/tap*' or 'Someone with black hair whose name sounds like *tap/tap.*'

* Start by recognising the rhythm in children's names. Play the 'Name Game' or 'Talking Drums', clapping the rhythm of each child's name in the gap.
* Try singing the register. Encourage the children to sing their reply as a solo.
* Use a two-tone drum or two different pitches on a xylophone to show how the pitch of the voice changes. This is called intonation.

Word Rhythms

* Clap the rhythm of well-known nursery rhymes and songs as you sing them. Choose three or four popular and contrasting rhymes and challenge the children to identify them when you clap the rhythm but don't sing the words?
* Choose two words from your current topic with different number of syllables such as pear and apple, car and lorry or ant and spider. Make picture cards and help the children to make up word patterns to chant. Try 'ant spider ant spider' or 'spider spider spider ant'. Add some longer words - dragonfly and caterpillar.
* Play 'Bubbles'. Draw two rows of circles or bubbles on a big sheet of paper. Write or draw a picture in each eg 'ant' or 'spider' and then chant the words. Ask a child to 'pop' one of the bubbles. This is now a 'silence' or rest. Carry on chanting and making 'silences' until there are no words left!

 *is for Sheep*

Sing Along String

Continuing a rhyming string helps children to listen for similar sounds in different words. This helps with analogy (using their knowledge of one word to help to decode another).

Try some of these:

* Sing some echo songs such as 'I hear thunder' or 'Frere Jacques' and repeat each line lots of times gradually getting quieter.
* Start with one word and sing the 'Rhyme Train' song together. The first child to think of a rhyme joins the train and stands behind with hands round the leader's waist. What is the longest rhyming train can you make?

The Rhyme Train

Join on the rhyme train.
Just think of a new rhyme.
Say it, clap it, play it, tap it.
Don't get out of time.

To: My Old Man's a Dustman

Rhyming Strings

* Play 'Catch a rhyme'. Sit in a circle, and start by saying a simple three-letter word like 'cat', 'log' or 'pig'. Throw the ball to a child and ask them to choose a rhyming word. They throw the ball to a friend who has to think of another rhyming word.
* Thread a button, big bead or reel onto a long piece of string and tie the string in a loop. Sit in a circle and ask everyone to hold onto the string. Pass the button around in time to Button on a String. At the end of each repeat the child holding the button can add a rhyming word. Nonsense words should be accepted.
* Sit in a circle and start a steady clapping beat. Start with a simple word (cat, sit, jam etc) and go round the circle with everyone adding a rhyming word. It doesn't matter if children repeat a word or make up a nonsense word - listening to and saying the rhyming words is the important bit!

Catch a Rhyme

Can you catch?
Can you throw?
How many rhymes
do you know?

Button on a String

Button, button, on the string,
Travel slowly round the ring,
If the button stops by you
Sing a word, or rhyme or two!

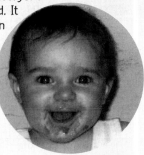

Hearing and saying initial sounds in words

* Explore sounds that children can create using different letters. Try humming long 'm' sounds, or singing long vowel sounds, and repeating short consonant sounds such as 'bbbb' or 'pppp'.
* Try making a 'Stormy day sound story' using these sounds: a few gentle raindrops ('t' 't' 't'), gradually getting faster as the rain gets heavier. Pouring rain ('sssshhhhh'). Rumbling thunder ('ggrrrrr' or 'crrrrk'). Lightning flashes ('sssttt' or 'zzzzz'!).
* Let the children make up their own sound picture of space, a fairground, the seaside or the jungle.
* Use a toy microphone and pass a sound around the circle. Encourage children to use their voices imaginatively to make different sounds. Use letter sounds and nonsense words.

Letter Sounds

Make a Sound

Leaping leopards, roar, roar, roar,
Leaping leopards, roar, roar, roar,
Leaping leopards, roar, roar, roar,
Roar, roar, roar in the jungle.

Sneaky snakes, hiss, hiss, hiss,
Sneaky snakes, hiss, hiss, hiss,
Sneaky snakes, hiss, hiss, hiss,
Hiss, hiss, hiss in the jungle.

Continue with:
Galloping gibbons, ooh, ooh, ooh,
Furry fruit bats, eek, eek, eek,
Crazy crickets, chirp, chirp, chirp,
Pretty parrots, squawk, squawk, squawk,
Cranky crocodiles, snap, snap, snap,

To: Skip to My Lou

Initial Sound Songs

Some simple songs to help children to recognise initial sounds.

Changing the sounds rap

Can you change bat into something you wear?
Can you change pig into a hat of fake hair?
Can you change dog into a very misty day?
Changing the sounds, that's the way!

Can you change bug into a comfortable mat?
Can you change wet into a cute dog or cat?
Can you change hen into one more than nine?
Changing the sounds, that'll do fine!

Do You Know the Letter?

Do you know the letter 'a',
The letter 'a', the letter 'a'?
Do you know the letter 'a',
Then sing along with me.

Ant and apple start with 'a',
The letter 'a', the letter 'a',
Act and ankle start with 'a',
So sing along with me.

To: Do you Know the Muffin Man?

Initials

If your name starts with a 'j'
Come and join in.
If your name starts with a 'j'
Come play the drum.

To: Lavender's Blue

Alphabet Sounds

Recognising the letters of the alphabet: Try some of these:

* Sing through the alphabet to the traditional tune 'Twinkle, Twinkle, Little Star' and any other versions of alphabet songs the children are familiar with.
* Have fun making different sounds and actions for each letter of the alphabet. Or sing some of these:

The Alphabet Song

A B C D E F G,
H I J K L M N O P,
Q R S, T U V,
W, X, Y and Z
Now I know my ABC,
Next time you can sing with me.

To: Twinkle, Twinkle, Little Star

Singing Sounds

Choose a letter,
Choose a letter,
Make a sound,
Make a sound,
Sing it altogether,
Sing it altogether,
Sing a sound,
Sing a sound.

To: Frere Jacques

Alphabet Sounds

Aaah, Boom, Crash, Ding, Eeek,
Flick, Goo, Honk, Icy, Jingle,
Klink, Lah, Moan, No, Oops,
Pop, Quack, Rattle, Sigh, Tick,
Ugh, Voom, Whizz, XXXX, Yawn,
Zoom!!!

The Acting Alphabet

A is for acting
B is for bouncing
C is for coughing
D is for dancing
E is for eating
F is for falling
G is for galloping
H is for hopping
I is for itching
J is for jumping
K is for kicking
L is for laughing
M is for moving
N is for nodding
O is for opening
P is for pointing
Q is for queueing
R is for running
S is for singing
T is for talking
U is for understanding
V is for vrooming
W is for wriggling
X is for x-raying
Y is for yawning
Z is for zigzagging!

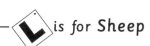

is for **Sheep**

More rhymes and songs to help rhythmic awareness.

Tasty Sandwich

Tasty sandwich, tasty sandwich,
What shall I put in my tasty sandwich?

Juicy jam, honey roast ham.
That's what we'll put in a tasty sandwich!

I hear you mutter peanut butter!
That's what we'll put in a tasty sandwich!

Just a trickle of tasty pickle!
That's what we'll put in a tasty sandwich!

Cheddar cheese, oh yes please!
That's what we'll put in a tasty sandwich!

Adding Sounds

Add a sound and change the word,
It's so easy I have heard.
Add a 'b' in front of 'all',
Then you've got a bouncing ball.
Add a 'c' in front of 'at',
Then you've got a curious cat.
Add a 'd' in front of 'or',
Then you've got a dusty door.
Add an 'f' in front of 'ace',
Then you've got a funny face.
Add a 'g' in front of 'oat',
Then you've got a granny goat.
Add a 'h' in front of 'air',
Then you've got some healthy hair.
Add a sound and listen well
How many new words can you spell?
To: Hush, Little Baby

Robots in a Ring

Three robots in a ring, in a ring,
Three robots in a ring, in a ring,
As they beep and whirr
and turn and do a spin,
Three robots in a ring, in a ring.
To: Heads, Shoulders, Knees & Toes

We Are Aliens

Aliens, aliens,
We are aliens,
Speaking sounds,
As we travel round the world.
Ooooooo chka chka chka.
Ooooooo chka chka chka.

Crowded Bathtime

In my bath along with me,
There's quite a crowd, as you will see.
With any luck, I can play with my duck,
You can hardly see the water!

In my bath along with me,
There's quite a crowd, as you will see.
I turn a pot into a yacht,
With any luck, I can play with my duck,
You can hardly see the water!

... And then I wish for my blow up fish...
... My submarine is very clean...
... I take the plunge and find my sponge...
... I use my soap that's on a rope...

CVC Song

My cat is very fat,
My cat is very fat,
E I addy oh
My cat is very fat.

The dog lay on a log...
The pig is in a wig...
A bug fell in my mug...
My hen sat in her pen...
I tried to cut the nut...
To: A Hunting we will Go

The Rhythm Train Rap

I'm riding in the runaway train,
Diddly-dum, diddly-dum, diddly-dum, dee.
Up the steep hill and down again,
Diddly-dum, diddly-dum, diddly-dum, dee.
Through the forest, thick and dark,
Diddly-dum, diddly-dum, diddly-dum, dee.
By the corn fields and past the park,
Diddly-dum, diddly-dum, diddly-dum, dee.
Round the sharp bend and into the town,
Diddly-dum, diddly-dum, diddly-dum, dee,
Using the brakes, slowing right down,
Diddly-dum, diddly-dum, diddly-dum, dee.
Station lights are blinking at me,
Diddly-dum, diddly-dum, diddly-dum, dee.
Home at last and there's the sea,
Diddly-dum, diddly-dum, diddly-dum, dee.

L is for **Sheep**

Tailpiece

The message of this book is that although all the writers would acknowledge the key role of phonics in learning to read, there are many factors that practitioners need to take into account when considering when to embark on a more formal programme of phonics teaching, particularly one where children work in large or whole class groups.

Deciding when, how and in what context such programmes should begin should not involve you in looking at the calendar, even though you may be encouraged to use the child's fifth birthday as a universal marker. Everything you will have read in this book will tell you that the decision is much more subtle, involving factors which relate to the individual nature of each child.

Each child has a unique brain. Each child is born with a hundred thousand million brain cells, and each of these is capable of linking with twenty thousand others. Babies and children make these links in their brains faster and more effectively in a stimulating environment. We now have convincing evidence that the ideal environment for learning of any sort is full of movement, hands-on experience and contact with others; an environment where young brains and bodies can practice both listening *and* responding, movement *and* control, looking *and* touching, freedom *and* order, stimulation *and* consolidation.

So keep it active, keep it fun

Even children who have had a rich early environment with their parents or other key carers will still develop at different rates. Individual differences in the development of physical, social, neurological and cognitive skills, all essential for the development of early reading, remain into puberty and beyond, and are intimately entangled with a child's gender, their prior experience, the language spoken in their home, and their additional needs for physical or learning support. As children move from the security of early care, we must ensure that the rich diet of talk, listening, stories, rhymes and poems continues to feed their brain development as the physical environment continues to develop their bodies.

So take account of prior experience

Children who live and play with engaging and supportive adults, who experience singing, dancing, music and rhyme, who have time to explore the world with their own bodies and at their own level, who are encouraged to be active, to ask questions, to solve problems, to use analogy to extend their learning, to listen carefully and to speak clearly and confidently may be ready for a systematic programme of phonics by the age of five. For those who have not had such advantages, the wait will be longer.

So encourage key learning skills

However, there are five groups of children who may well, despite such a supportive culture of early literacy, take more time to achieve this level.

- children who have English as an additional language (many of whom are learning two languages at the same time)
- children with learning or physical difficulties and disabilities (whose physical, cognitive, social or neurological development may be delayed or damaged)
- children who are born in the summer months and therefore are the youngest in their year group (just because they are younger than the others!)
- children who may have had a discontinuous, disturbed, dislocated or distressing time in their young lives, or who may have been coping with stresses that affect development
- many boys, because their hearing and speech development is often slower than that of many girls.

So remember the exceptions and keep expectations high

Knowledge of and sympathy for the difficulties of these groups of children must not result in abdication of our responsibilities, or an approach which could result in failing to help *all* children to succeed. Such knowledge must encourage practitioners to examine the ways in which phonological awareness develops, and to continue to offer lively, engaging and purposeful activities for all children which take into account *both* their age and their unique stage of development.

So match your support to individual needs

Practitioners also have a responsibility to use their knowledge of child development and of the individual children in their care to ensure that managers of schools and settings understand that professional judgement, rooted in observation of individual children must be supported when pressure is applied to start too early on formal programmes, where children are expected to use skills which they have not yet developed.

So make it a whole setting/school issue

The latest chapter in the debate about how to help children learn to read will not be the last. Conscientious practitioners, teachers, parents, researchers, writers,

advisers and politicians will continue to search for the Holy Grail of universal reading – and everyone who already can do this complex, challenging and rewarding activity wishes the day would soon come when every child could learn to read without anxiety, pressure or fear of failure. Until that day arrives, trust your professional judgement, know the children you work with and remember that laughter, enjoyment, fun and music help us all to learn, whoever we are.

Sally Featherstone: Tailpiece

Glossary

analytic phonics

    involves the analysis of whole words to detect phonetic or spelling patterns. The sounds of letters are taught in the context of words, and children learn to break words down rather than build them up. Its supporters argue that this is a more logical approach than building words up from isolated sounds and an efficient way to help children develop a large sight vocabulary for reading and spelling.

beat competence

    the ability to pick up (or create) and maintain a steady beat. Research indicates that the development of beat competence is important in a wide range of learning activities, including learning to read.

blend

    to combine individual sounds together to sound out a word; e.g. the sounds c-a-t blended together, make the sound *cat.*

brain gym

    a therapeutic re-patterning programme originally designed (by Paul Dennison in the 1970s) to help children experiencing learning difficulties. Brain gym uses simple physical exercises and movement to stimulate mental activity and promote learning.

cluster

    two (or sometimes three) letters making two (or three) sounds; e.g. the first three letters of '*str*aight' are a consonant cluster.

digraph

    two letters which together make a single sound; e.g. *sh, ch, th, ph, ee, oa.*

grapheme

    a letter or a group of letters representing one speech sound; e.g. the *f* in *full*, the *ph* in *photo*, and the *gh* in *cough* are all written representations of the same phoneme.

graphophonic

    concerned with the relationship between letters and sounds, the sounds that the letters in the alphabet make and the way in which words are written and spelt.

morpheme

    an element of speech or written taxt which has a meaning or grammatical funtion that cannot be broken down any further; e.g. *out, go* and *-ing* are morphemes of *outgoing.*

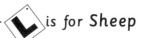 is for *Sheep*

onset

the initial sound (phoneme) that starts a word; the remainder of the word after the *onset* is called the *rime.*

phoneme

the individual speech sound in a language that serves to distinguish one word from another. The combination of phonemes that make up a word is what distinguishes it from other words, and therefore enable it to be understood.

phonemic awareness

the concept that every spoken word can be seen as a sequence of phonemes, and that phonemes can be represented by letters of the alphabet.

phonics

a method of teaching people to read by training them to associate letters and combinations of letters with the sounds they make (their 'phonetic values') and using these sounds to create words.

phonological awareness

defined in the Rose Report as 'the general ability to attend to the sounds of language as distinct from its meaning'.

rime

the remainder of the word which follows the onset – often referred to as the 'rhyming' part of words which rhyme.

scaffolding

term used to denote a structured framework (e.g. model, guidance) provided by the teacher to support the learner in acquiring new skills. The scaffold is removed as the learner becomes confident and competent in the new skill.

semantic

relating to the meanings of different words or symbols.

syllable

a unit of sound that is, or makes part of, a word; e.g. *moth - er* has two syllables.

syntactic

relating to the grammatical relationship of words and morphemes in sentences.

synthetic phonics

starts by teaching an awareness of phonemes, mapping these to letters and then showing how the sounds of letters can be blended (synthesized) to produce different words. Supporters argue that this is a more systematic approach than that offered by analytic phonics and is therefore an easier route for children to follow.